Gethin

The Product Innovator's Handbook

How to design and manufacture a product that people want to buy

First published in Great Britain by Practical Inspiration Publishing, 2023

ISBN   9781788604208   (print)
          9781788604222   (epub)
          9781788604215   (mobi)

This book gives you the information you need to design and manufacture your own successful product. However, it can't give you the insights, research and good judgement that are relevant to your particular situation. Those are down to you. Happy inventing.

Every effort has been made to trace copyright holders and to obtain their permission for the use of copyright material. The publisher apologizes for any errors or omissions and would be grateful if notified of any corrections that should be incorporated in future reprints or editions of this book.

Want to bulk-buy copies of this book for your team and colleagues? We can customize the content and co-brand *The Product Innovator's Handbook* to suit your business's needs.

Please email info@practicalinspiration.com for more details.

FSC
www.fsc.org
MIX
Paper | Supporting responsible forestry
FSC® C013604

Contents

Introduction

Maybe you were cooking dinner, taking a shower, or putting up a shelf. You might have been at work, grappling with a problem that's been bugging you for years. You could have been chatting with a friend, listening to their tale of woe. Or maybe you were walking the dog. And it came to you out of the blue: 'There must be a better way to do this.'

That's how products are born. You experience a problem and have an idea for a gadget or device that will solve it. When that solution is out in the world, it will give you the satisfaction of having created something lasting and meaningful, and – if you've done it properly – it will make you money. The wonderful thing about developing a product is that it fulfils so many of our desires. Whatever you want to achieve in life – creating an income, learning something new, helping people – it's a way to do it all.

Right now, though, it's still in your mind's eye. You can see it on a shelf; you can imagine people talking about it and recommending it to their friends; and you can envisage it making their lives easier and more enjoyable. But it doesn't exist yet. Coming up with an idea is the simple part – it's turning it into a commercial success that's the challenge. One of the misleading things about the product marketplace is that we don't see the inventions that *didn't* make it into the world – the ones that never got produced, or flopped as soon as they hit the shelves.

Products that don't sell aren't necessarily badly conceived or designed; there may be other reasons, such as having too little investment or poor market positioning. There are so many disciplines that you have to master to create and sell a product – from research and manufacturing to fundraising and marketing. Yet you don't know what you don't know. Were you aware, for instance, that a 3D CAD model alone rarely provides enough detail for a manufacturer to make your product? That your idea might infringe someone else's intellectual property? That there are ways of selling your product that will make you more money than others? Or that there could be a fundamental flaw in your idea that will only become apparent after it's produced? It's rare for anyone to be an expert in all these areas.

I'm the founder and Managing Director of ITERATE, a product design consultancy, and I've been designing products for over 15 years. In that time, I've witnessed pretty much every pitfall on the product development journey. From concepts that aren't technically feasible and designs that aren't patentable to ideas that are plain unworkable – they've all crossed my path. On the other hand, one of the joys of my job is carrying products through to completion, enabling them to improve people's lives, make a difference in the world, and generate a healthy income for their owners.

I've learned that there's a lot you need to think about if designing a product is going to give you what you want. That's why I've written this book – to present you with a toolkit for making your product a success. You'll learn how to tell the difference between an idea that has potential and one that's a dud; methods for strategizing your product so that you design and sell it in the right way; what to do about protecting it through patents and design registration; useful information about funding and manufacturing options; and how to choose the right designer for you.

We start with why you want to embark on the exciting and sometimes perilous journey of creating a product in the first place because this will form the basis of all the decisions you make. We'll then explore whether your idea solves a genuine problem, and who for – otherwise it runs the risk of sitting on the shelf rather than being the runaway success you were hoping for.

Next, I'll outline the options for protecting your intellectual property and how you're going to fund your venture. Once you've pinned that down, we'll look at how you're going to manufacture, market, and sell it. Will it be made in China or the UK? Is it best to sell it direct or via a subscription? And is there potential to license it to a branded retailer, or would putting it online be best? There are so many different options, and choosing the right one for both you and your product is fundamental to your success. Finally, you'll learn how products are designed and what you should look out for in a good designer to give your product the best chance of being a winner.

Along the way, you'll receive valuable inspiration in the form of stories and examples. You'll read about products that worked, products that didn't, and – most importantly – the crucial factors that made the difference. Only a minority of products designed make it all the way to market, and still fewer sell in high enough numbers to make the investment worthwhile, so anything you can learn from other people's experiences is useful. Many of these stories are those of ITERATE's clients. We take confidentiality seriously, so I've taken great care to protect the technical and commercial sensitivities of the people and products involved.

A new product journey begins with the first step, so let's get started with the first decision you need to make: why you want to design a product in the first place.

1

Know Your Why

Developing a new product can be really exciting. You're about to realize a dream that you might have held for a long time, and one that could even make you wealthy. Not only that, but you'll be creating something that will make a difference in the world. Something you can point to and say: 'I did that.'

But it's also a journey filled with challenges – technical difficulties, funding let-downs, marketing complications, and more. The nature of these challenges is dependent upon the kind of product you want to create, with some being more testing than others, but even the simplest ideas rarely go according to plan. There are always hurdles to overcome before you see your product on the shelf. That's why you need to know your reasons for embarking on this journey – your 'why'. If you don't understand your why, you may be tempted to give up when you receive poor feedback from a potential customer, or your patent agent gives you bad news. On the other hand, if you know your motivation, you'll gain strength from it; it will give you the drive to carry on.

There's also another, more practical, reason for knowing your why, which is that you'll make better decisions about your product as you go through the design process. There are many forks in the road when you create something new, and you'll often find yourself needing to choose which direction to go in. If you're clear on what you want to achieve with your product, you'll be able to choose between options quickly and confidently, whereas if you're unsure, you'll spend a lot more time considering what to do for the best.

To help you tap into what your why could be, I've identified four types of product creator. They're not intended to cover every person, but they're based on my experience working with many different clients over the years; as such, I think they're pretty accurate. Take a look at them and see if you recognize yourself.

The dreamer

You're at the top of the game in your career and you're respected for your achievements; your kids are grown up and you have money to spare – everything is looking positive. Yet there's something missing. Surely there's more to life than meetings, spreadsheets, and deadlines? Is that all you have to look forward to until you retire?

Then it appears: the idea. You're going about your day when you realize that, if only you had a particular tool, you'd be able to solve a problem in a way that makes life easier, more fun, or more practical. You do your research and discover that no one has come up with this idea before. Are you really the only person to have thought of it? It seems that you are. You feel a jolt of excitement, the like of which you haven't experienced in years. Could it be that you're the one to make this product? Imagine, one day, walking into a shop and seeing it on the shelf, knowing that you put it there. Now you have a dream to make a reality.

For you, it's not so much about the money but the achievement. Yes, you'd like to make a return on your investment, but far more valuable is the satisfaction of having created something tangible that you feel a sense of ownership over. Not only is it fun to show it to your friends and family, but you also get to learn about how products are designed, manufactured, and sold. It's as if you've gained a whole new dimension to your life.

Peter had a similar dream to yours. He came to us with an idea that was simple but effective: a clip to prevent the pages of a book from flapping in the wind when you're reading outside. The unique selling point was that it incorporated a folding mechanism, so it could be used as both a bookmark and a book holder. This allowed the reader to keep their place, hold the book in one hand, and read it without interference, all in one go. For Peter, the satisfaction was that he could put his device into the world and be responsible for it from beginning to end. He worked with us to design it, got it manufactured in China, sold it via his website, and managed all of his own social media. It brought him a small but steady income, which is exactly what he was after. He had no aspirations to build it into a larger business by developing other products to create a range because all he wanted was to keep enjoying his invention.

This example shows how your 'why' for creating a product can influence the decisions you make about it. Peter was driven by the desire to see his product out there. He wanted the great feeling that came every time he received an email with an order; for him, it was all about having it done. Because his product idea was a relatively simple one, he was able to start producing and selling it within a year. If, on the other hand, he'd envisaged something more technically complex, he'd have had to wait a lot longer to see his dream fulfilled. He might have ended up feeling frustrated about how long it was taking and lost heart. As it was, he was delighted with what his creation added to his life with just a few months of work.

The learner

You're similar to the 'dreamers' in almost every way bar one, and it's a way that probably isn't obvious to you. Like them, you have a fantastic idea for a product that will solve a problem, so you work with a design consultancy to develop a first prototype. However, here's where you diverge from the 'get it out there' approach that dreamers have. When the amended version of your prototype comes back, you see more you'd like to change, then more, and more again; the cycle repeats itself almost indefinitely. That's because your motivation is more about having a fascination with how products are designed than it is about making something and selling it.

Geoff was one such 'learner'. He'd seen how difficult his elderly mother found it to put on her coat when she went out. With her co-ordination and flexibility impaired, she could get one arm in a sleeve, but she struggled with the second arm. As a software developer, Geoff was a natural problem solver, so he came up with an idea for a hook device that would make it easier for her. His plan was that if she found it useful there would be many others who could also benefit – he'd spotted a product opportunity.

When he came to us, we could see that there was potential in his idea and worked with him to create a series of concepts and prototypes. At first it went well. Geoff loved learning about how we designed new products and he made a concerted effort to understand the engineering behind them. But as a detail person he became obsessed with every step of the process, and it became apparent that no version of the product would ever be completely right for him. After several years of this, he came to the realization that his 'why' wasn't to make something that could be sold, but simply to enjoy the process of designing it. His meetings with us were like a hobby or a day out for him, rather than being part of a commercial journey.

The professional

You're a trained expert, such as a doctor or scientist, and have spent years in your chosen field. In the course of your work, you've spotted an opportunity to develop a product that will enable you to help more people, deliver better outcomes, or carry out your job more easily (maybe all three). While you certainly want to make money out of the product, your main motivation is to support your professional work and maybe even make a name for yourself at the same time. Not only that, but if your idea will save the health service money or benefit it in some way, it makes strong commercial sense to go ahead with your plan.

We've worked with many professionals who have had aspirations like these. A great example is Reza, a medical specialist who approached us with an idea for a device that would analyse the urine of patients with a certain chronic illness. The idea was that they'd keep it at home and use it to test themselves on a weekly basis. If the machine flagged a problem, they'd have enough notice to adjust their lifestyle, and this would avoid them having to go into hospital – something they'd normally have to do several times a year. As you can imagine, not only would this be a life-changer for the patients, but it also represented a huge potential cost saving for the health service.

While it seems that this product should have been an obvious success, it's actually a good example of how things can go wrong during the development process. The device looked great and worked as it should, but during the testing phase it transpired that the assumptions underpinning it weren't as robust as Reza had initially thought. This wasn't something that he could have known about ahead of time, as it was only ever going to emerge during live trials. All was not lost, though. He then started testing the product for the detection of other types of early stage diseases – another valuable usage. This was much more successful and still economically worthwhile because it would prevent people from having to undergo invasive tests. It wouldn't be suitable for home use, but consultants could keep it in their surgeries as a way of diagnosing such diseases quickly and at low cost.

However, this new route didn't work out in the way our client hoped either – although for different reasons. The investors who'd bought into the original idea became nervous about the pivot and withdrew their support; without funding in place, the product couldn't survive. This was a blow, but let's remember that Reza's motivation was to help people through his work. Surely there was another way? There was. He ended up creating a joint venture with a medical supplies company, the investment from which enabled his product idea to become a reality. This shows how important it was for Reza to know his 'why'. His product journey required remarkable persistence, which he had in abundance because he had a burning desire to make his patients' lives better.

The trader

You work in an organization that already creates and sells products and you're wanting to expand your range. Or maybe you're in a non-product-related job and looking for a side hustle that you can eventually turn into a new career. Either way, you see creating and selling a product as a commercial proposition. For you, it's not about whether your idea is exciting enough, but whether it will sell at a profit. How much will it cost to develop? What are the timescales to market? And how many units might you trade? Not only that, but what other products could you create alongside it – does it have the potential to spawn a number of related items that would make up a credible range?

Unlike with the previous types of product creator, your idea could be highly innovative, a twist on an old favourite, or anything in between. That's because it's not so much about the concept as the reality of the marketplace. I'll give you a couple of examples so you can see what I mean.

Andrew came up with an idea one morning when he was hunting for his keys yet again. Late for work, he cursed the fact that there was nowhere convenient and secure to put them when he came home. When he thought about it, he realized that the perfect solution would be a holder that hung from his banister, so he tried a couple of home-made options. One was made of cloth, which wasn't sturdy enough, and the other was made of rigid plastic, which was unstable. He'd seen what was, at the time, a new flexible plastic that was being used to make baking trays and thought that would be perfect. So he worked with us to create a key holder out of that material and managed to get it into some homeware retailers, where it flew off the shelves. While this product may not have had the lofty purpose of a medical device, and its innovation lay solely in its material, there's no denying that it was a commercial success. It certainly satisfied Andrew's desire to gain a profitable return on his investment.

Another example of a 'trader' is Stuart. He came to us because he had spotted a gap in the market for a particular type of kitchen bar stool. The interesting thing was that he'd discovered this by analysing online sales data and trends for different stools that already existed. One type was selling £8 million worth of units per year, and the other £10 million. If he could create something that sat between the two, he was confident that he could achieve a similar return.

It was a calculated risk, but one with a clear potential financial reward because Stuart had something to compare it to. As you can imagine, the product would have been of no interest to a 'dreamer' or a 'learner', but to him it was an opportunity that he grasped with both hands.

You can see that if you're a 'trader', you'll probably make quick decisions that are commercially driven because you want to start making money from your product as soon as possible. You'll also think longer term than you might if your motivation was related to enjoying the process of product creation. For you, it's all about the return on investment.

What's your why?

Each of the whys that I've described are valid in their own right – there's nothing to say that you have to be one type of creator or another. But it is worth being honest with yourself about what your primary motivation is because not only will you find it easier to make decisions about your product, you'll also be more likely to feel satisfied with the results.

For instance, if you're mainly driven by the desire to see your gadget on the shelves as quickly as possible, you'll want to create something that's not too complex but still unique within its market. There would be no point in you trying to develop the next generation vacuum cleaner, for example, because there would be too many technical challenges involved. If you're a doctor motivated by the desire to develop a device that will benefit your patients, you'll see simplicity as being of secondary importance to effectiveness and reliability. And if you want to create a product that enables you to enjoy the design process, you won't want to take on too much financial risk because you'll be unlikely to see a return on your investment.

If you're still finding it hard to work out which type of product creator you are, try this exercise. Imagine you're going through each stage of the process in turn and take note of how you feel as you go along. Here's a top-line list of the key phases (which in practice don't always happen in this order – but let's keep things simple for now).

1. Identifying a problem and coming up with a solution for it
2. Gaining feedback from the people you hope will buy it
3. Visualizing concepts for your product
4. Testing a functional prototype
5. Getting your product manufactured
6. Marketing, selling, and distributing it
7. Benefiting from your newly earned riches

When you read that list, which stage or stages gave you the biggest buzz of excitement? When you came up with the idea? When you saw it brought to life in a prototype? When you sold it? If you found stage 6 to be most intriguing, you could be a dreamer or a professional; if it was stages 3 and 4, then you're probably a learner; and if it was stage 7, you might be a trader. Of course, there are many crossovers between them, but this will give you a good steer.

To me, a product is something that's meant to be sold – it's a tool for generating revenue. That doesn't mean you can't enjoy the process of designing it and putting it out there, but it does mean that you should consider how much you're prepared to invest in it, and for what likely return. It all comes down to what you want to get out of it.

Now that you know your why, in the next chapter we'll explore what problem your product will solve. This is the crucial first step in evaluating your initial idea.

The main points

- ✓ Developing a new product is exciting, but your motivation to see it through to the end will be stronger if you know which aspects of the process you're going to find most enjoyable.
- ✓ Dreamers are driven by the idea of creating something new in the world.
- ✓ Learners love to immerse themselves in the product design process.
- ✓ Professionals are motivated by the desire to create products that help them in their work.
- ✓ Traders want, above all else, to earn money from their products.
- ✓ It's important to keep commercial realities in mind when embarking on your product journey.

2

What Problem Are You Solving?

'I've had an idea for a product that will mean my patients can treat themselves at home, rather than them coming into the clinic.'

'I'm a keen walker, but what always annoys me is how bad hiking rucksacks are for my posture. I've come up with a unique strap attachment that fixes the problem.'

'I've thought of a way to make cleaning carpets easier; I reckon it could be a money-spinner.'

This is why I love picking up the phone in our office – I never know what idea I'm going to hear next. Every call reminds me of the endless creativity of the human brain and of the limitless capacity we have to be enthusiastic about our inventions. It also makes me think about how important it is that every new product should solve a problem. Of course, it's possible to create something that simply looks nice rather than addresses a need, but it would be more a work of art than a product. If you want to develop something that's of use, problem solving is the most logical place to start in my opinion.

This is, however, where many product creators go off track. They spot a problem and, instead of fully exploring it, they jump straight to the solution. It's the way our minds work. We're visual creatures, which means that, as soon as we can mentally see a way of dealing with an issue, we tend to fixate on that rather than on the problem we began with in the first place. The downside of this approach is twofold:

- As soon as your attention is off the problem and on the solution, you've stopped asking yourself whether the problem represents a viable market opportunity.
- It's easy to miss potential solutions that might work more effectively than the one you've thought of.

This chapter encourages you to think differently about the problem your product is solving. What if you were to hold the problem up to the light and examine it from all angles? Would it still seem painful or widespread enough to be something that people would want to spend money on solving? And is your idea for dealing with it really the best one? Just as there are many ways to skin a cat, so there are countless ways to solve a problem; it might be that there's a much better option just waiting to be discovered.

How successful product creators come up with ideas

I talk to many people who have ideas for products, and the ones who go on to create successful products are usually those who've had a personal experience of the problems that they solve. For example, we've worked with many surgeons and medical personnel who've come up with solutions to problems that their patients face in the course of their treatment. They know their patients well and, through working with them day in and day out, have had ideas for devices that can help them. Other people have a light-bulb moment while going about their job or taking part in a hobby or activity; they think of a way that they could enjoy it more or find it easier, if only they had a particular gadget to use.

We receive a lot of enquiries from first-time parents who've come up with ideas to make looking after their babies easier. This points to an interesting aspect of having an idea, which is that it's often having a *new* experience that instigates it. During the Covid-19 pandemic, when everybody suddenly had to work from home, we received many requests to do with designing fitness products or related to home working. We also heard from people interested in creating ways to maintain better hygiene or different types of face masks. It was fascinating to see how so many people were thinking in the same way at the same time, all because they were living different lives from normal.

Another way that people come up with ideas is through deliberately going out and looking for a problem to solve. If they do their homework thoroughly, this can be an excellent way of coming up with a commercially viable product. One such example is Chris, who came to us on behalf of his consumer healthcare company. He'd spent a lot of time browsing through the funding platform Kickstarter, monitoring trends on which types of products were successful at winning funding. He noticed that there were many businesses launching air-quality monitors, and that they were raising huge investments. The monitors were portable devices, designed to be worn or clipped to bike handlebars or a bag, that gave out real-time readings of the amount of pollution in the air. Users could then choose to take a different route or avoid an area altogether.

The issue that Chris could see on Kickstarter was that most monitors were taking far longer to launch than had originally been promised. And the reason? They were all designed to work with smartphone apps, and it was the process of making the apps work with the monitors that was causing the delay. So Chris asked us to develop a device that didn't need an app. He could include one later as an additional feature if he wanted, but for now his aim was to get the product out there so that it could start to secure a brand following. We therefore created a design concept for an air-quality monitor based on existing technology, which meant he could launch it more quickly than those that were funded at the time. It sold really well, and the company has now created a range of related items aimed at its new audience.

This way of identifying an opportunity – by looking at what is and isn't working in the market already – works especially well if you have a commercial mindset and want to develop a product that you can be sure will sell. In fact, it's another reason why people use crowdfunding platforms, which are not just for gaining investment but also for testing the viability of an idea. We've found this ourselves when we've worked with clients who have launched working prototypes of their products online; they've gained a lot of useful market feedback.

What was the basis for your idea? Did it come from personal experience, in which case you now need to validate it with the people who might buy the product, or did it come from market analysis, which means that you now need to work out if there's a true gap in the market?

The relationship between problem and solution

It's not enough for your product simply to solve a problem – it has to do it in *at least one* of the four following ways. It must help people to:

- Do something more quickly or efficiently
- Do something more easily or in a more enjoyable way
- Do something more cheaply
- Have a lower environmental impact
- Save money in itself by being cheaper to buy than the alternatives

Think about which category your solution falls into. Does it help people to carry out a task with less hassle so that they can reduce the amount of time and energy they spend on it? Pretty much every domestic appliance you own has been designed to meet that need, as have many of the tools you use for work. Or does it enable people to do something with more ease or pleasure? Everyday examples that spring to mind are TV remote controls or home medical testing kits that prevent a trip to the hospital.

Alternatively, does your idea help people to save money, like Soda Stream does for those who enjoy fizzy drinks, or screen protectors do for people who might drop their phone? Or is its unique selling point that it's cheaper than its competitors? This is the weakest way to solve a problem because, in any market, there can only be one lowest cost option and it will only be a matter of time before someone undercuts you.

Ask yourself how your product will help people to solve their specific problem. If it offers more than one of the benefits above, that's a sound starting point for success. But if you're struggling to put it into any of these categories, you may have come up with a solution that's in search of a problem. You'll be unlikely to make a commercial success of it and might want to revisit your plans.

When a problem isn't a problem

If people don't perceive there to be a strong enough need for your product (in other words, they don't think they have the problem it's designed to solve, or they don't think it's painful enough), they won't buy it. So even if you reckon it would make their life easier, or cheaper, or more fun, you're going to find it difficult to sell it to them.

This is what Ashok found when he developed a clip that stops shoelaces from coming undone. He was often annoyed by the problem when he was out and about, and he assumed that it must affect many other people as well. After canvassing a few of his friends and family, who all agreed with him, he worked out a way of stopping the laces from unravelling by attaching a fastener to the top of the shoe. He then spent a lot of time and money on getting the product developed and manufactured, only to find that few people wanted to buy it. Why was that? Because, to most people, shoelaces coming undone is just one of those things. If you ask them whether they find it a problem, they may say yes, but it's not important enough for them to buy a gadget to stop it happening and attach it to their shoes every time they go out.

This shows that a problem is only ready for a solution if enough people think it's an issue. There's no doubt that Ashok's invention worked and was innovative, but for him to make it a sales success he'd have had to persuade a lot of consumers that something they saw as a minor inconvenience was a burning issue. That's hard work, and not always possible.

Innovation or improvement?

Another way of thinking about the problem your product is solving is to ask yourself whether your solution represents something completely new in the market (an innovation), or whether it's an advance on something that already exists (an improvement). Each has its pros and cons.

Innovation

The advantage of coming up with a product that's completely new is that you'll be the first in the market with a radical development. It will be hard for others to copy or undercut you on price, and you can establish yourself as the main player. That means you'll have a longer-term opportunity to make money from it than if it was an improvement; think of how Tesla has done this with electric cars, for instance.

However, there are disadvantages to this approach. You'll have to work hard to persuade people that they need your product because it often involves them having to change the way they carry out the activity it's related to. When mobile phones first came out, for instance, it took people a while to go from seeing them as being for emergencies to using them every day. If your product involves such a shift, it will take time and marketing spend to make it happen.

Improvement

The advantage of creating a product that's an improvement or variation on what already exists is that it's lower risk. You can analyse the sales data for what's already out there and calculate what your likely return on investment will be. This will help you to know what inventory to order, how your costs will stack up, and where you should price your product in relation to others. You can also produce and sell it more quickly because you won't have to innovate from scratch or persuade people that they need it in the first place.

The downside of this is that your opportunity is likely to be shorter lived than if you created something new. It won't take much for a competitor to launch something better or cheaper than your version, and you may find yourself having to reduce your price or find another way for your product to survive.

A product that we once developed shows both approaches at the same time. We were asked by a business that sold sleeping aids to make one of their items more environmentally friendly. It was a device for people who snore or have sleep apnoea, and it looked a bit like a gum shield. The user would dunk it in boiling water as a one-off precursor to fitting it to their teeth, then, when they went to bed, they'd put it in their mouth and it would stop them snoring during the night. It was (and still is) highly successful and sells extremely well.

The challenge we were asked to overcome was to remove the need for the plastic tongs that were supplied with the mouthpiece for when it was put into boiling water. The company didn't want to ask users to use their own cutlery, for instance, so what was the alternative? With active input from our client, we came up with the idea of creating a storage box with a dimple in the underside that the user would clip the device into. They'd then sit the box on top of a cup of boiling water with the mouthpiece suspended below, lift it off when ready, and no tongs were needed. Depending on how you look at it, this was either an innovation or an improvement. It was an innovation in that it was a completely novel solution to the problem of needing the plastic tongs, but from the perspective of the product as a whole it was an improvement.

You may be wondering which route to take: innovation or improvement. As we explored in the last chapter, it comes down to your motivation. If you want the excitement of creating something unique and you're willing to do whatever it takes to make it work, then innovation is for you. But if you want to start making a return on your investment as quickly as possible, then improvement is the best option to consider.

Why you need feedback

When Apple launched the iPad, the initial response was mixed. Die-hard Apple fans queued outside stores all night to buy it, while others questioned the need for a product that hovered between a smartphone and a laptop. After all, nothing like it had existed before – it was natural for people to wonder whether it was solving a real problem or whether it was just another expensive gadget. However, as we know, it didn't take long for consumer confidence in the Apple brand to overcome the reluctance to try something new, and the tablet revolution was born.

The point of the story is this: while Apple can launch an innovative product without doing comprehensive market research and people will still buy it, most of us lack Apple's brand loyalty and marketing clout. When we 'normal' people develop products, we need to ask its potential users what they think. If we don't, we risk making something that won't sell. That's why you need feedback, right from the start.

Do you know what the target market for your product looks like? Who are your typical users? And have you spoken to any of them (family and friends don't count)? It's important not only to know who you want to buy your product, but also what they think of the idea as a concept. And yet so few product creators do this, usually for two reasons:

- They're afraid that someone will steal their idea
- They're worried that the feedback will be negative

Both concerns are understandable, but let's take a look at them more closely. In my experience, ideas are almost never stolen. That's because the value isn't in the concept but in the execution of it. In fact, there's nothing to say that thousands of people might not already have had the same idea as you, but, because they lack the will, the confidence, or the money to make it happen, it stays in their heads. There's a famous quote that is often attributed to light-bulb inventor Thomas Edison but was probably coined by academic Kate Sanborn: 'Genius is 1 percent inspiration and 99 percent perspiration.' The people who put their products out there and make money from them are those who turn inspiration into action – and that's you, not the people you talk about your idea to. In addition, there are various ways in which you can protect your idea, even while you carry out research; we'll go into these in a couple of chapters' time.

Regarding the fear of negative feedback, this is part of human nature. Until you tell people about your idea, it's safe. You nurture and cherish it, imagining a great future for it, until the day comes when you hold it up to the light and someone says, 'Well, it's okay, but I'm not sure I'd use it.' What a crushing blow. But negative feedback is just as valuable as positive because it can make your product better. It may be that your solution isn't comprehensive enough, but it could still work if you make a few tweaks. Even if the feedback is overwhelmingly poor, it doesn't mean that your idea is a write-off. If you seek to understand why it's not working for people, you can probably turn it into something much more compelling. So many people think that it's all or nothing with their ideas, but the reality is that it's rare to come up with the perfect solution first time.

It's not only important to gain feedback on your initial idea but also on your designs and prototypes as you go along. Each time you show people something that's more refined and 'real', you're able to draw better conclusions from what they say about it. So when you have your sketch concepts and 3D models, show them to the kinds of people your product is intended for because they'll be able to see themselves using it. And when you have your first working prototypes, you're in a position to receive the best quality feedback of all.

If you're worried that people will dismiss a non-finished version that looks a little rough and ready, please don't be. We had one client who came up with a device to help brass music teachers and their students to play their instruments more quietly while in lessons. Rather than a mute, which can distort the sound, it was a soundwave blocking device that the teacher could switch on. This prevented the noise from travelling outside the room, but it didn't affect what the teacher and student could hear. The inventor didn't want to research his initial idea to gauge interest, as he was worried that somebody would steal it. He was also reluctant to show the prototypes to other teachers because the early versions looked a little clunky. By the time he felt ready to reveal it to the world it was pretty much finished, but then came the disappointment. Although the product worked well, it turned out that not only were there too few interested teachers to support a viable production order, it wasn't portable enough to be practical, either. If he'd known this from the beginning, or even during the development process, he might have been able to create something that more people would buy.

Looking at the positive side of gaining feedback, you can think of it as making a product the 'Lean Startup' way (see Eric Ries' book of the same name if you're interested to learn more). You're putting something out there that isn't perfect, gaining feedback on it, and using this feedback to refine and improve the product. The idea behind this is that you end up with something that people want because it's based on real-life research.

We took this approach when we developed a product for our client Emile. His business identified a need to monitor people's movements when travelling in groups, such as for teachers running school trips or tour guides shepherding tourists around foreign countries. The device he came up with was a piece of wearable technology that could be used over two or three days without needing to be recharged (existing solutions were too power hungry for that). We decided to take a working prototype to the Consumer Electronics Show in Las Vegas – a huge event where all the big technology brands display their new ranges. Emile took a stand there to showcase his product, the purpose of which was twofold. It enabled him to gauge interest to see if it had enough sales potential (it did), and it also gave him the opportunity to attract potential investors. In a way, the stand was like a face-to-face version of Kickstarter, combining feedback on the product with buy-in from investors. We also recorded video testimonials from people talking about the product, which allowed Emile to create marketing collateral that he could show to investors back home.

Is your market big enough?

Once you've gained feedback from people in your target market, you have validation for your idea. It tells you that you have a recognizable problem to be solved and that your solution addresses it. Your next task is to broaden that into estimating how many units you can sell and at roughly what price. This represents the scale of the problem your product is solving.

Are you on the low-volume/high-value scale or the opposite? In other words, do you expect to sell a small number of products at a high price or a large number at a low price? There are a couple of methods you can use to determine this.

Benchmarking

If your product is a variation on one that already exists, you can obtain market data from sources such as company reports, Amazon sales, and subscription tools. These give you a feel for how other similar products are performing. Even market research and trend analysis reports can tell you what the market is worth and which companies are selling what volume of units. It's unlikely that you'll come to a definitive figure through this, but you should be able to gain a level of confidence from the information. This is more difficult to do if your product is an innovation, but there are still items you can compare it to as a benchmark. Remember that, while your product may be better than what's already out there, it will also be unfamiliar, so you'll be selling against a brand and product that's well established. This will affect your sales volumes, at least at first.

Top-down estimating

If you know the total market for your product is worth 'x' and you might be able to capture 'y' percent of it, you can translate that into numbers. For instance, if gaining one percent of a £5-million market seems feasible, you're looking at a sales value of £50,000; if it's two percent of a £10-million market, your sales could be £200,000.

Bottom-up estimating

On the other hand, if your production cost is £50 per unit and you retail it for £100, you can work out how many you'll need to sell to hit a revenue of £50,000. Looked at from both perspectives, you can gain a sense of whether you'll sell enough units for your idea to be profitable. If it's a niche product, then you might still be able to make money out of it, but you'll have to raise your price. The key question is, will enough people want to make that kind of investment? And if it's a mass market item, you'll need to pitch the price at a relatively low level so as to capture all the sales you can. But can you still make a profit?

We worked with one entrepreneur, David, who'd spotted what he thought was a gap in the market for a lower-cost version of a dishwasher. He knew it was the kitchen appliance that people were most likely to forgo, and he reckoned that, if he could develop a bargain-basement version, he could enter the mass market with it. We carried out a market assessment to see how much it would cost to create a cheaper model. However, what we discovered was that the dishwashers already on the market were the price they were because they needed to be; it simply wasn't possible to create a cheaper version that would be safe and reliable. There was therefore no gap in the market, which was why the brands already selling the appliance didn't offer a rock-bottom-priced model in their ranges. In David's case, he'd spotted a problem that needed solving but missed the fact that the market was already being served in the best way possible.

In summary, the validity of your idea comes down to a number of factors. Does it solve a pressing problem that enough people have? Do those people perceive that they have this problem or is it only you who thinks that? Have you asked the kind of people who will use your proposed solution what they think of it? And do you have a feel for the potential market size so that you can estimate whether it's commercially viable? These are important questions to answer before you go any further. In the next chapter, we'll look at how you can learn more about the most important people in your world right now: your target market.

The main points

✓ Before you explore your product idea further, examine the problem that it's solving.

✓ Does your idea come from your own experience or from market analysis?

✓ There are five types of problem that your product can solve – which does yours relate to?

✓ Is your product an innovation or an improvement?

✓ You need to ask for feedback on your idea from the type of people who will use it.

✓ It's important to estimate your market size.

3

Who Are You Selling To?

Amari came to us because he suffered from arthritis. This made gripping handles difficult for him, especially when mopping and sweeping floors. He'd discovered a way to make his life easier by fitting a special moulded grip over the existing handle of a mop or broom. As well as having an easy-grip design, it also had a spur attached to it that meant the user's hand wouldn't slip down the pole while cleaning the floor. He called it the Rhyno handle.

Together we created a product that worked really well, and it became popular with other people who had the same disability. But most interesting of all was what happened next. Users started fitting the handle to other household items such as cooking pans, umbrellas, and wheelbarrows. And they weren't all arthritis sufferers; some were people who just wanted a more comfortable way of going about their daily lives. Eventually we adapted the inside curvature of the product so that it could accommodate different devices, and this expanded its customer base still further.

There are two reasons why I'm telling you this story. The first is that it's an excellent example of how having a tightly defined target market for a product is essential for its success. Amari initially chose to sell the handle only to arthritis sufferers like himself, and it did well. People could see what it was for and how it would benefit them, and so they bought it. If he'd created a versatile grip that anyone could use with anything, it would have been a lot harder for potential customers to see it as beneficial to them because there was no clear and obvious use for it. The second reason is that it shows how having a focused target market doesn't necessarily limit a product's sales – in fact, it can expand them. When people see that something is designed for a person with whom they don't identify, they don't necessarily rule it out for themselves. In a strange way, they find it easier to see themselves using it than if they weren't sure whether it was for them in the first place. This shows that it's a product's *customers* who will define how it's used, not its *inventor*.

This is why you need to know what your target market is and understand it well. Yet I often find that when I ask people who they envisage selling their product to, they say something like, 'Men aged between 20 and 50.' That's a start, but they need to drill down a lot deeper than that. In this chapter you'll learn how to create a persona for your ideal customer, so you know exactly whom you're aiming at. Because when you have a distinct idea of whom your product is for, you'll be much clearer in your thinking all the way through the development process – from the design brief and deciding what features to include to what the product should look like and how to manufacture it. It's also just as crucial when it comes to your marketing because it will help you to direct it towards the most appropriate people.

Before we go any further, I'd like to remove a fear that holds many creators back from developing successful products; namely, if you define your target market too tightly, you'll not appeal to the mass market and will limit your sales. Hopefully you've seen from Amari's experience that the opposite tends to happen. Developing something that's for 'everyone' means that you'll not do the best possible job of solving the problem your product was designed for, whereas making it for a specific audience enables you to focus all your activity on your customers' needs. Think about how it is for you when you buy something new. What would you rather have? A product that seems like it would solve a problem for you but you're not entirely sure, or one that you're certain is exactly right for your specific needs?

This is where identifying the problem you're solving and whom you're solving it for become intertwined. You've already learned about the problem part in the last chapter, so now let's look at the people who want the solution: your target customers.

How to define your target customer

Here are some helpful techniques that you can use to create a persona for your ideal customer. It's best if you split the process into two stages:

1. Information about your target customer and their life
2. Information about the other products they already buy

Your target customer and their life

In this, you're building a rich picture of the type of person whom you envisage loving your product so much that they're irresistibly drawn to buying it. I suggest that you put a lot more detail into this than you might originally have planned and think about all the relevant aspects of the person's life. Here are some ideas for what to focus on:

- What they look like (it's helpful if you can find a picture of someone who fits the bill)
- Their age and gender
- How much they earn
- What they do for a living
- How educated they are
- Who they know and how they communicate with them (such as online social media)
- What industry they work in
- What tools they need to do their job and manage their lives at home
- Their biggest challenges in life and work
- What they enjoy doing in their spare time
- Their day-to-day habits, both in relation to your product and in general
- The things that they see when they go about their day, both in relation to your product and in general
- The feelings that they have about those things

Your first thought might be, 'But how can I know all these things about a person? They're not even real.' That's okay, all you're doing is using your common sense to come up with the best answers you can. The purpose of the exercise is to start thinking in depth about whom you want to make your product for, not necessarily to come up with a description that's realistic in every way. If you know someone who fits the bill, even better – you can use them as a template.

Put your person into a short document and keep it to hand so that you can refer to it throughout the design process. We also encourage our clients to create two or three target personas because different user groups may be attracted to different aspects of your product. You can see an example persona that we've created at www.iterate-uk.com/example-persona.

Your target customer and the products they buy

When you're clear on exactly who your ideal customer is, think about the other products they already buy. This will help you to decide on a design direction for your product; in other words, you're asking yourself whether it would look 'at home' in their life.

As an example, we developed a device that looked like a set of headphones, but rather than for listening to music it was for helping people to meditate. We wanted to build a picture of what it would need to look like if our target customers were to think it was 'for them', so we created a set of mood boards. The first showed products that were designed to be worn on the ears or head, like ours would be. The second displayed products that were wearable technologies. The third showed items with a range of different shapes and forms that we thought our customer would enjoy, even if the purpose was different. And the fourth had pictures of products with colours and finishes that we predicted would appeal to our target user. We included watches, kettles, thermostats – anything that gave us a feel for what they valued in their life.

You can take this route or you can simply think more widely about the kinds of things your customer already buys. What mobile phone do they use? What car do they drive? What gadgets do they own? Not only will you build a picture of how your product fits into their lives, you'll also gain a sense of what they value visually. Do they like smooth curves, sustainable materials, bright colours, touch-screen displays? What themes can you see in terms of what they find attractive?

Bear in mind that you're looking for overall trends and commonalities here. If you're too specific when you look at other products, you might be tempted to assume that because your target customer likes a lot of white items, for instance, then your product should also be white. That can limit you. What you're aiming to do is identify themes; these could be related to functions, shapes, colours, finishes, or anything else that recurs often enough to jump out at you.

Gaining feedback from your target customers

In the last chapter we explored the importance of asking your ideal customer what they think about your idea. Here we take it a step further because before you design your product you need to do some in-depth research with your target customer group. The more intelligence you can gather at the beginning of your project, the better your product will be. You'll be able to convert your assumptions into facts that you're confident about and amend your designs to suit. If you create a persona without validating it, it's only your best guess at what people want. Research makes it real.

The main research techniques that I tend to use are interviews, observational studies (in which you watch people doing things that relate to your product), questionnaires, and focus groups. I'm not suggesting that you do all of these, but choose one or two that would give you the feedback you need. It's possible that you'll discover you've made some wrong assumptions about how your product will help people, and that's fine. Now you have the chance to change your idea so that you're better able to translate your customer's problem into what your solution should look like.

We went through this process after we identified a gap in the market for a sustainable shower head. Although you might not think of shower heads as being environmentally unfriendly, the truth is that the vast majority have a surprising number of parts inside – about 20 or 30. There are springs, seals, and plastic elements welded to one another, few of which are recyclable. It's a product that's been around for a long time, and nobody has done anything innovative with it for years.

Having come up with the idea, our next step was to define our target customer. For that we created a questionnaire. The answers revealed that, while shower heads often have a range of water jet patterns for different shower experiences, most people only ever use one of them. They also revealed that, while they feel the need for a choice, they didn't necessarily want to change the setting on the fly. This helped us to refine our design approach because it meant that we could strip out the internal complexity by incorporating only a single face plate into the product; in fact, we reduced the total number of parts to three. And to offer the choice that people said they wanted, we made the face plate removable and replaceable with others that we included in the box. We called our shower head MOHONTO, and it went on to win a European Product Design Award.[1]

This shows that it's only when you talk to the types of people who will buy your product that you can see how they might use it. Another example of this is when we were in the early stages of developing a device for people with severe breathing difficulties. We knew that people with this condition also tend to have certain other medical problems and are often of a similar age, so we carried out some one-to-one interviews. We wanted to see what people with this condition thought of existing competitor products so that we had the learning upfront before we did our own development. The main insight was that many of these people also had arthritis, and because of this they struggled to use small buttons and interfaces to control the device. This was really useful, teaching us that we needed to make the buttons larger and the interface simpler than we would otherwise have

---

[1] You can read more about it here: https://iterate-uk.com/portfolio-item/mohonto-shower-head

assumed. It was a discovery that we could only have made by talking to the right people.

When a customer isn't a customer

There are some products that aren't designed to be bought by the person who will use them, such as gifts, products for children, or those bought by organizations on behalf of their employees. Not only that, but, if you sell your product to retailers rather than direct to consumers, you have to consider what the retailers will think of it. They might, for instance, reject it because the box it comes in takes up too much space, whereas the end user wouldn't see this as an issue.

One company we worked with made custom shoes for people with medical problems that prevented them from fitting into commercially available footwear. It didn't sell the shoes direct to the end users but to the health service, which was purchasing them on their patients' behalf. Orthotists would measure the patients' feet and send the results to the health service, then the health service would ask our client to make the shoes. There were therefore three separate parties in the chain.

Suppose we were to design a foot-measuring device that was superior to the one the orthotists already used – one that employed lasers, for instance. That would be great for the shoe wearer because it would cause them less discomfort and great for the health professionals doing the measuring because it would be quick, easy, and accurate. But would the health service buy it? Their requirements would be different. Their main concerns would be to do with price, the reliability of supply, and the potential need to train the orthotists who use the product. So we'd have three personas to create: the health service buyer, the health professional, and the end user (maybe even two or three for the latter).

This shows that your target customer isn't always as simple as you might think. What range of people does your product idea need to appeal to? And which characteristics do they consider to be most important? Here are some ideas to get you started when you're thinking about what your customers value.

End users

- Ease of use
- Aesthetics
- Price
- Features
- Functions

Buyers who aren't end users

- Price
- Size
- Reliability of supply
- Longevity of product
- Appeal to end user

Have a go at creating your own lists of concerns for your various personas; you might find it revealing when you see the differences between them.

The connection between features and profit

I often find that when people have an idea for a product, they're keen to add every feature possible to it. In their understandable enthusiasm to make it a success, they want it to cover every potential use that their target customer could put it to. However, consider the cost implications of doing that. If you add eight features rather than two, and the product ends up costing £10,000 to make rather than £5,000, you're unlikely to sell it for a high enough price to make a profit. Instead, think about the one or two functions it must have for people to buy and enjoy using it. These are the ones that will make it a profitable success.

Suppose you have an idea for a Bluetooth speaker. You could add a clip that allows your customers to attach it to a bag or belt so that it can be used when they're out and about. That might be useful for some, but what impact would it have on the cost? Would more people buy it because of the clip, or would they have purchased it without one? Try to attach a monetary value to every feature you include; this is difficult to do, but it's a great discipline when you're prioritizing.

Much of your decision-making will come down to your target audience. If you're aiming the speaker at people who spend a lot of time outdoors, for instance, they might find the belt clip to be an essential feature. But if you're aiming it at teenagers who want it for their bedrooms, the clip would be redundant (and even off-putting). Also, do your potential customers want the complication of having lots of features? Every time they use your product, they'll have to decide which features to use and which not to; this can affect how much they enjoy it. Many inventors assume that the more functions you cram into a product the better it will sell, but a more constructive way of thinking about it is to ask yourself what your user will value and whether you can deliver it profitably. And don't forget that limiting your features allows you room to create future versions of the product, or even a range of them, each with different elements.

Going back to our foot-measuring device, what possibilities could there be for this? We could include a rechargeable battery at extra cost, but does it need one? Maybe a disposable battery is acceptable. Or what about an instruction manual or a carrying case? All these are additions that would have to be paid for, and if they aren't going to increase the product's sales, are they worth it?

You can see how this focus on profitability links to establishing your selling price, which in turn is related to how much you will spend on manufacturing your product. We'll go into this in more detail in Chapter 7, but it's worth starting to think about it now. You won't know for sure what it will cost to make until you have a finished design, but you can consider how much your target customer would be willing to spend on it.

You've made a great start. You've identified why you want to create your product, the problem it solves, and the people who are most likely to buy it. In the next chapter we'll look at how to protect your intellectual property so that your hard work benefits you rather than someone else.

The main points

- ✓ Identifying a tightly defined audience for your product, and gearing all your decisions around it, maximizes the chance that your product will sell.
- ✓ That's because you'll create something that a core group is irresistibly attracted to, rather than a product that could appeal to anyone.
- ✓ When defining your target customer, think about what kind of person they are and also what they already buy.
- ✓ Ensure that you gain feedback from them so that you can validate or change your product idea.
- ✓ Work out what features your target customer really wants, rather than adding everything you can.

4

Protect Your Product

When you originally came up with your product idea, what was the first thing you thought of doing? I'd be willing to bet that it was protecting it from being copied by anyone else. That's only natural – you don't want to spend precious time and money developing something only to see it being ripped off by a competitor. Taking out a patent, for instance, can seem like an obvious first step, but, as you'll discover by the end of this chapter, it should actually be one of the last.

Before we go into that, let's explore the whole notion of what's called 'intellectual property' (IP). This is the innovation or originality in your product – the thing that makes it unique – and by protecting it you stop other people from using it. IP protection is a hugely specialized area, and many legal professionals make a handsome living out of it. My perspective on it isn't a legal one, but it is based on years of experience working with clients who use IP protection in their businesses. I see when it works well for them and when it causes major problems, and I've learned that the key to reaping the benefits from it is to use it in a strategic way. It's the area of creating a product that there are the most misconceptions about; my aim here is to debunk the myths so that you can make informed decisions about whether, and how, to protect your IP.

There are four main types of IP protection:

- Copyright
- Trademarks
- Design registration
- Patents

Quite often, when people speak to me about their product ideas, they're not sure what type is applicable to them. They ask, 'Can I copyright this design?' or 'Can I patent our logo?' It's important that you understand the purpose and relevance of each kind of IP protection so that, when you talk to people who can help you with it, you're using the right terminology. The two areas I'll spend most time on are design registration and patents, as they're the ones that are most relevant to product design, but first I'll give a brief outline of copyright and trademarks.

Copyright and trademarks

Although you almost certainly won't need either of these to protect a product innovation, it's still worth understanding what they are so that you can see how they might fit into your overall business strategy.

Copyright

The term comes from its literal meaning: the right to copy. It's applied to pieces of creative work such as writing, music, and art, and the interesting thing is that you don't have to apply for it, you automatically hold it by being the creator of the work. Copyright protection doesn't cover ideas, procedures, processes, systems, or discoveries, nor is it possible to copyright a product design. So while you can apply the © symbol to your marketing literature, for example, you can't use it to protect your product.

Trademarks

A trademark can be used to protect any word, phrase, symbol, or graphic design that identifies your goods and services, such as your brand name or logo. It can take one of two forms: unregistered and registered.

Unregistered trademarks are denoted by the ™ symbol that you might have seen beside logos, for instance. Anyone can use this symbol if they want and it has no significant legal force attached to it. It's just a way of claiming that this company or person was the first to use a specific name or graphic design. Should someone infringe your unregistered trademark, you'd have to prove that you were the first to use it, which is not always easy.

If you really want to protect a brand name or logo, you need to register your trademark by going through an official process; this gives you legal recourse if someone was to use it for their own purposes. For instance, we've registered our company name ITERATE, which gives us the right to use the ® symbol next to it. Only we are allowed to use ITERATE as a trading name in association with the specific purpose for which it's been registered, and in the territories that we've chosen.

Like copyright, a trademark can't protect a product design. It might be useful for your company name, brand name, or logo, but it has no relevance to the product you make. For that you need either a design registration, a patent, or both – and these are what I'll cover next.

Design registration

This is a relatively recent form of IP protection, which is probably why many people don't know about it. As a result it's underutilized, which is a shame, as it holds many benefits compared to taking out a patent.

So what is it? It's a way of registering the *look* of your product. This includes the appearance, the physical shape, the configuration (how the different parts of the design are arranged together), and the decoration. Note that it doesn't include how your product works or any aspect of it that's not to do with the external aesthetics.

You can register your design by going to www.gov.uk/register-a-design. Once it's processed you have the right to prevent anyone else from using it for up to 25 years, although you have to renew your registration every five years.

Design registration pros

- It's quick, simple, and low cost. Registering a design will only set you back £50 and the process is straightforward. All you need to supply are line illustrations of your product in multiple orientations, and that's it.

- It's usually successful. We've never had an application rejected, as it doesn't go through the same level of interrogation that a patent does.
- You can apply for a design registration retrospectively. So if you put your product on the market and it's successful, you still have the chance to protect it as long as you do so within 12 months.

Design registration cons

- Because the process for approving a design registration isn't as thorough as for a patent, the value of design registration lies more in protecting your design against being copied than it does in ensuring that you're not infringing someone else's design.
- It gives you a level of confidence that others will be unlikely to copy you, but not at the same level as a patent. However, a design registration can act as a deterrent.

The experience of Trunki manufacturer Magmatic Ltd is a good example of the pros and cons of design registration; this pivotal case has changed the way that many product developers now handle the process. The Trunki is an animal-themed, ride-on suitcase for children, the design of which was registered when it was first developed. So when a Chinese manufacturer started importing a lookalike product into the UK, Magmatic took it to court. Initially Magmatic won its case because the two designs were similar, but after several rounds of legal battles the final ruling was that the aesthetic differences were significant enough for the Chinese version to be legally sold. As a result, many product designers now register not only the design they intend to go to market with but also a number of variants. It's possible to file up to ten versions of the same product, so this makes sense as a protective measure.

Patents

A patent is a monopoly right to stop other people from making a copy of your invention and using it. It relates only to the territories in which you've registered it, and it lasts for 20 years after the date of filing. A patent can protect many things: a software programme, a unique recipe, or a process (such as a manufacturing procedure or a way of carrying out work). But from the perspective of a product creator such as yourself, it's of most use when you want to protect the IP of a mechanism that is part of your product.

To apply for a patent, you're best advised to use a patent attorney, who's a legal professional trained and experienced in this area. They'll make sure that your claims are robust and clearly articulated, and they will send it off for assessment. It can take a year or more to be awarded a patent – we even worked with one company whose patent took seven years to be approved, although that's extreme. In the meantime, you can label your product with 'patent pending', during which time you can put it on the market. You can have a patent pending for 12 months, which gives you breathing space to research your invention further and decide whether you want to finalize the patent (it's at that point that the major costs kick in). This gives you a year of being able to use your patent application as a deterrent, even if you decide not to keep it in the end.

If you'd rather avoid the extra cost of hiring a patent attorney, you can write your own patent application and file it direct; this might be the best route if you only want to put people off copying your design. But if you want to use a patent strategically as a way of gaining investment or selling your company, you're best to use a professional.

Some people applying for a patent are concerned that their product idea might unintentionally infringe somebody else's patent. There are a couple of ways to deal with this. One is to use Google's patent search function,[2] and the other is to search the website Espacenet,[3] which gives free access to over 130 million patent documents. These are good starting points to see what's already out there. I suggest that when you're choosing keywords for your search you use ones that describe the function or purpose of the product, as patent titles don't feature brand names. Also, be aware that there are many ways of describing the same function, and two similar product ideas can be described differently depending on who applied for them.

If your initial research throws up a lot of registrations, you might want to ask yourself whether

---

[2] https://patents.google.com/

[3] https://worldwide.espacenet.com

you want to go ahead. If you do, you can speak to a patent attorney. They'll be able to see what a particular patent is protecting and whether your idea is different enough from what's already registered.

Patent pros

- Because a patent isn't easy to obtain, it's a robust deterrent against people copying your innovation. They'll have to spend money on working out how to get around your protection.
- A patent is usually essential if you want to raise investment, license your product, or eventually sell your business. Venture capitalists and business acquirers are always asking for patents, and if you don't have one you might find it impossible to progress any further.

Patent cons

- You have to be able to demonstrate that what you've created is an innovative step; no one else can have developed anything that's the same.
- It's costly; you'll be unlikely to see much change out of £10,000 as a minimum, especially if you use a patent attorney. And if you register your patent in multiple territories, you'll pay a lot more.
- Your product design or prototype must not have been in the public domain before you apply for a patent. That means you can't apply

for it retrospectively like you can with a design registration, nor can you show it to people as part of your market research without asking them to sign a non-disclosure agreement (NDA). This can limit the feedback you gain, which is a crucial element in ensuring that you make a product that will sell.

- Because it takes a long time to have a patent approved, it can have a negative impact on when you launch your product. If it's commercially important to bring it out as quickly as possible, applying for a patent might not be the right thing to do.

Is applying for a patent the best step for you?

The protective power of patents was something that I witnessed first-hand while supporting a client on their stand at the Consumer Electronics Show in the US.[4] One of the other stands in our zone was occupied by a Chinese company displaying a one-wheeled electronic skateboard. One day, word went around that its stand was being stormed by three US marshals, who stripped away its products and promotional material. The next day, the owners of the company were hauled into court for patent infringement.

It turned out that a Silicon Valley start-up, Future Motion, had already patented its own one-wheeled electronic skateboard in the US; in fact, it held

---

[4] www.theverge.com/2016/1/7/10733946/future-motion-electric-skateboard-raid-ces-2016

two patents: one for the technology and one for the design. So when Future Motion learned of the Chinese company's plan to exhibit a similar product at the US show, they sent a cease and desist letter. Receiving no response, they gained an order from a judge to shut down the Chinese stand.

This shows that patents do work as a way of protecting your product from people who want to take advantage of your hard work and inspiration. What's more, for some products aimed at a global market in the medical, aerospace, automotive, and consumer electronics sectors, you wouldn't dream of going ahead without one. This is especially the case if you want to gain investment for your business or sell it one day because a patent is something tangible for investors to hang their hat on. In fact, many start-ups have the value of their product's IP as one of their key performance indicators; a patent adds to that value, which means the business can fundraise at a higher level.

However, the main problem arises when people don't see a patent for what it is: a statement that a design is innovative and unique, nothing more. A patent doesn't validate an idea or guarantee any level of commercial success, nor does it suggest that anyone will want to buy the product it relates to. A patent agent only looks to see if an invention is novel compared to everything else that has already been filed; they don't know (or care) if it's the best solution to a customer's problem or even if the problem exists at all.

So rather than thinking of a patent as a way of judging whether your idea is any good, ask yourself if your target market will value it. You should never use the awarding of a patent as a substitute for researching your design, or you could end up making a product that people don't want to buy. This is where a design consultancy comes in and why it's best to consult one well before you apply for a patent. A good designer will be full of ideas that you might not have thought of about how to make your product look better and work more efficiently. They'll find ways of creating more IP in it than you originally assumed was possible, and they can even work original IP into the design as part of the process.

Can you see what might happen if you applied for a patent before you talked to a designer? You'd have a dilemma. You'd either have to go ahead with a product that's not as appealing as it could be because you've already patented it, or you'd have to write off the costs of the original patent and start again. That's why, in my opinion, applying for a patent should be one of the last things you do, not the first.

Robert came to us with an idea for a household product that he'd already gained a patent for at a cost of £10,000. He wanted to create an income stream that would eventually support his family, as he was seriously ill at the time. I had major reservations about the viability of his innovation in the marketplace, but, being of the view that there's no such thing as an unworkable idea, I thought of ways to turn it into something more meaningful. The problem was that it would cost more than Robert could afford, given the money he'd already sunk into the patent. He had to walk away from an innovation that might have been successful if he'd gone about it in a different way.

Another area to watch out for is the number of territories you apply for. I remember watching an episode of *Dragons' Den* in which a teenage boy demonstrated his invention: the Boot Buddy.[5] It was a water bottle and brush combination that people could use to clean muddy boots. During the presentation it transpired that his mother had spent nearly £150,000 on patents in 22 different territories, an admission that drew gasps of horror from the dragons. This almost amounted to worldwide protection for a product that was unlikely to sell in more than a couple of geographical areas. You need to ask yourself what your business strategy is when you're deciding how many territories you want to be covered. Being realistic, where do you plan to sell your product? Will you really gain distribution all over the world, or is your home market (plus one other) more likely?

Do you need to protect your IP at all?

In the excitement of developing a product and gaining a design registration or patent, it's easy to forget that IP protection is only worth having if you're willing to enforce it. Given that it would involve suing someone or taking them to court, you can imagine how the costs would rack up. Of course, the deterrent is still there whether or not you choose to do anything with it, but it's a factor to consider.

---

[5] You can see it here: https://youtu.be/XEat0PL1eiE

In the end, I believe that your choice as to whether or not to protect your design largely comes down to your 'why'. If your aim is not to build a business but simply to create a unique product and put it out into the market, you don't necessarily need to spend a lot of money on patents – especially when you consider the time delays they can cause. There's a huge value in being the first to market with a product you've been able to gain broad feedback on without the limitations of NDAs. Are you sure a patent is really worth sacrificing that for? Even if someone does copy you, you'll still have first mover advantage and a more loyal customer base than your competitor, something that's especially valuable if you create more products in the future. Remember, a patent won't make your product a success in itself.

There are many misconceptions about IP protection and also lots of ways in which you can use it strategically to get the results you want. So before you go ahead with that patent application, consider whether it aligns with your 'why', and make your decision based on that.

In the next chapter we'll look at the crucial topic of money. How much of it will you need and where will you get it from?

The main points

- ✓ The main forms of IP protection that relate to physical products are design registration and patents.
- ✓ Design registration is a relatively quick, low-cost, and easy form of protection that is often

    overlooked. However, it's limited in what it covers and isn't as robust as a patent.

✓ A patent is essential for some products, sectors, and business objectives. It's also a stronger deterrent to competitors than a design registration.

✓ However, it's expensive, time-consuming and – if applied for in the wrong way and at the wrong time – potentially damaging to your product's success.

✓ Think of your 'why' when deciding whether (and how) you need to protect your IP.

5

Fund Your Product

While your product idea holds a huge amount of potential, its value comes from making it happen in the real world. And yet to do this takes money – a surprising amount of it. It's easy to underestimate how much you'll need to invest, not only in design but also in manufacturing and marketing. In fact, the most common reason for a product not getting to market isn't that the idea is unsound, but that the project has run out of money.

So you need to factor in your costs right from the start and think about how you're going to pay for them. Over the years, I've worked with many clients who've used various fundraising methods for their product development; through this I've learned which methods are most suitable for which types of products and their creators. My aim in this chapter is to give you a feel for how much money you'll need to spend and also to shed light on the main sources of finance.

How much money will you need?

Asking how much it will cost to make your idea a reality is a completely reasonable question to ask, but unfortunately not so easy to answer. Your budget will depend on a wide variety of factors, such as whether there are electronics in your product, how complicated the internal mechanisms are, and whether it needs to comply with industry standards. However, in the interests of giving you something to go on, you can treat the following as a rough guide.

Your first tranche of spending will be on the design and prototyping. The investment here depends on which design consultancy you work with and how technical and challenging your product idea is, but at ITERATE our average charge is between £50,000 and £150,000. If it's something highly complex, such as a medical device, it might be upwards of £250,000.

Then come your manufacturing costs. These usually make up a more significant investment than the design because manufacturing involves tooling, which can be expensive; this means it will probably cost between two or three times that of the design. You'll also need to commit to minimum order quantities of 5,000 to 10,000 units from the factory. And if your product includes electronics, you can assume a minimum order of 10,000 units, given the investment in making the printed circuit boards, the plastics housing them, and the assembly.

After that you need to factor in your marketing, sales, and distribution costs. These will depend on how you intend to make your target audience aware of your product, and also on how large or heavy your product is to store and despatch. And let's not forget legal costs, which will be significant if you apply for a patent.

Does all this give you pause for thought? Are you starting to wonder if you want to create this product after all? I'm sorry if I've brought you down to earth with a bump, but it's better to know the facts now than to launch into the process and run out of cash part way through.

The good news is that, if you're committed to making your product a success, there are several ways in which you can raise the money you need. The four main sources of finance are:

- Self-funding
- Crowdfunding
- Government grants
- Venture capital

Self-funding

This is self-explanatory – simply use your own money to fund your product. As you can imagine, this has both advantages and disadvantages.

Advantages of self-funding

First of all, it's quick and easy. There are no forms or applications to fill in, no meetings to arrange with people who might (or might not) give you money, and no hanging around waiting to hear if you've been successful. You can get on with your product without delay, which means you'll start making money from it more quickly too.

Self-funding can also work well if your product doesn't need a high level of investment to get it to market. If the technical complexity is low and it's reasonable to assume there will be few challenges in the design and manufacturing, this might be the best option. If you cast your mind back to Peter, whom we met in Chapter 1 with his special bookmark for reading books outside, he funded his product himself. The speed and ease of using his own money, and the full ownership this gave him of the entire process, was part of what made it enjoyable for him.

Disadvantages of self-funding

With any new product development there's always a degree of uncertainty because you don't know what problems you'll encounter. Anything could happen – someone may contest your patent, the internal workings of the product might be more problematic than predicted, or you may receive negative feedback during your research and have to rethink your approach. This is when costs can spiral out of control and you could find yourself in a compromising position.

That's why I'd never recommend self-funding a product if it has anything more than a low level of technical complexity because it will take an awful lot of capital to get it to market and your chances of unexpected costs are high. I recently spoke to someone who was planning to put the money he'd saved for a house deposit into developing a product, and this made me very nervous. While I know the potential pitfalls because I've seen them happen time and again, they're not always obvious to someone who's going through the process for the first time. What if this guy lost both his money and his dream of a buying a home? How would he feel then?

To sum up, self-funding can be a great idea, but it can also be a dreadful one because you're liable for all of the risk. If your product is relatively simple and you have the cash available, you might want to go down this route. But if it doesn't sell as well as you predict, or you run out of money before you get it to market, you could lose your investment. Ask yourself if you're prepared for that to happen.

Crowdfunding

This is when you put your product onto an online crowdfunding platform and ask people to buy it before it's been made. The revenue you gain allows you to manufacture it, and in return you give your backers a better price than they'd pay after it's on general sale, along with other incentives if you want to. The two main crowdfunding platforms are Kickstarter and Indiegogo. Both work in similar ways, matching product creators with backers, but there's one crucial difference. With Kickstarter you set a target amount that you want to raise and only receive it if you attract the entire sum. With Indiegogo you keep whatever you attract, even if it's below your target, but you still have to supply the products. That means you'll need to find an alternative source of funding to make up the difference, if there is one.

In addition to Kickstarter and Indiegogo there's Crowdcube, which is suitable if you want to pitch your whole business rather than an individual product. There are also other platforms for crowdfunding appearing all the time; many are sector specific, so it's worth researching what's out there if you have a niche product idea.

Advantages of crowdfunding

Anyone can do it. You don't need to fill out a detailed grant application or convince sceptical investors to buy into your idea, you just need some enthusiasm, marketing flair, and a good feel for your target market.

We've worked with quite a few clients who've raised money in this way, creating working prototypes and videos for them to display on their crowdfunding pages. One was the inventor of a virtual reality locomotion controller, the VRGO Mini. This product enabled virtual reality gamers to have a more immersive experience by allowing them to tilt their bodies while sitting on a special cushion. We built a working prototype that the company used for its Kickstarter campaign, which was successful in reaching its target amount. This allowed the business to place a minimum manufacturing order and break even on its expenses.

However, crowdfunding isn't just about raising money; it's also about gaining exposure. Even if you don't raise the money you want, you can still take comfort from the fact that many people will know about your brand who didn't before. Some product creators use it primarily as a marketing tool; they set a deliberately low target that they know they'll have no trouble reaching just to get their audience excited about their idea.

Disadvantages of crowdfunding

The first disadvantage springs from the point above: while these platforms present themselves as fundraising tools, they actually operate more like marketing platforms. This is borne out by the terminology you'll find when you explore their sites, where words such as 'campaign', 'fans', 'communities', 'launch', and 'social networks' abound. It follows that, if you don't understand enough about marketing and promotion to make your campaign a success, you may not win the investment you need.

First of all, you have to create a compelling and professional video of your product and put together some persuasive marketing copy. Next, you need to have a pre-existing audience of potential buyers who will want to back it. Campaign timescales are short, so if you don't make enough sales within the deadline, your efforts will be in vain. This takes a lot of work in a concentrated period of time. As Kickstarter itself says, 'Expect the first few days after launch to be very busy as you spread the word to your community, answer questions from potential backers, and more.'

You also need a working prototype of your product to use in your video. This doesn't, however, need to be expensive – it's often possible to use 3D printing technology to create something that looks and functions like the finished article. You can then use your crowdfunding money to finalize it ready for production.

Crowdfunding tips

It's easy to think that crowdfunding is simply a matter of putting some information about your product on a website and waiting for people to back it, but that's the mistake many product creators make. It's a shame because if your idea is a good one then it deserves better than that, as one of our clients, who invented a new type of home security camera, discovered. He invested a significant amount of his own money in research and development and planned to raise enough through Kickstarter to fund the tooling and manufacture. The product was fantastic and worked incredibly well, but unfortunately his crowdfunding campaign was unsuccessful and he only raised £20,000 of the £50,000 needed.

So how do you give yourself the best chance of success? Here are some top-line tips that I've picked up from witnessing other people's campaigns:

- You'll only gain a minority of your backers from existing crowdfunding platform fans, so you need to generate your own as well. Contact your social media connections, work contacts, friends, and anyone else you know who might be interested. If you're a business with a customer base already, then this might be relatively easy, but if you don't have anyone to start off with, you'll find it hard.
- The campaign timescale is limited, so if you wait until it launches before you start spreading the word, you'll be too late. That means you need to build up an audience of willing customers before you launch. Many

people buy Facebook and Google ads to drive traffic to a landing page that asks for sign-up details to let potential backers know when campaigns are live.

- Think carefully about the target amount you set. On Kickstarter, aiming too high could mean that you don't receive any money, but aiming too low might not generate enough to make your product. On Indiegogo, you may win part of your funding but not all.
- Be prepared to spend a significant amount of time and effort managing and optimizing your campaign. Think of it as a part-time job from well before you launch until the end.

Crowdfunding is a fun, accessible, and often highly lucrative way of gaining funds, and there are many products that have been catapulted to success through it. However, it's not the silver bullet that many people think it is. You might have a fantastic product, but if your marketing effort doesn't match up, then you won't have the success you're after. If you want to take advantage of crowdfunding's benefits, the key is to approach it strategically and with a large dose of marketing know-how.

Government grants

This is an area in which we've had direct experience through our work with both Innovate UK and the Welsh Government. If your product is innovative and requires a significant amount of research and development, applying for a grant might well be the best route to funding. Grants aren't usually suitable if you're a one-person inventor, as you'll need to show a track record of achievement, but they are if you're part of a business.

Innovate UK

This is the main grant-awarding body in the UK and the most common source of research and development grant funding for businesses of all sizes. It not only offers grants but also loans and other forms of support; you can find out more at www.ukri. org/councils/innovate-uk.

The most interesting aspect of how it works is in the competitions it sets. For instance, the UK government might create one for new and innovative products to enable elderly people to live independently in their own homes. If your company could create such a product as part of its overall strategy, you'd be an ideal candidate to take part.

At ITERATE we've spent several years working with Innovate UK in various ways, starting with entering a product idea of our own into a competition. The contest was based on the theme of 'connected digital additive manufacturing', and Innovate UK was looking for businesses to develop advanced 3D printing technologies that could connect 3D printers around the world. If successful, it would be possible to ask a printer in one country to print a product in another, thereby avoiding having to ship it. To enter our bid, we teamed up with a 3D printer manufacturer, a company that could print electronics, and a local university. At first, we didn't have a clear idea about how we were going to work together, but we did know that with such a fantastic team we could end up with something amazing. It was the bidding process we needed to learn most about, but after numerous discussions we carved out a clear project plan and divided up our responsibilities. This enabled us to create a compelling bid.

In the end we won £1.1 million to develop a new 3D printing technology that could print plastics and electronics within the same machine – something that hadn't been done before. Today you can, if you were so inclined, buy one of these machines; they're mainly used in the aerospace sector, and the technology has opened the doors for similar products in the medical space. We had to fund part of the development ourselves, but we gained a healthy return on our investment and – crucially – an insider's knowledge of the competition process. We learned how to bid; what kinds of projects get funded; how to run a project of this complexity; how to report to Innovate UK; and how the body works. This experience has enabled us to help many clients who have projects that are suitable for funding in this way.

It's worth bearing in mind that there are also other grant-awarding bodies, such as those available through some universities. In particular, it's worth looking at the Catapult Centres[6] throughout the UK. These specialize in different areas of product development, and, if you work with them, they'll allow you access to various types of funding. There's

---

[6] https://catapult.org.uk

also a Knowledge Transfer Network (KTN) that sits alongside Catapult, which can be a helpful source of information.

Devolved government grants

If your business is based in Scotland or Wales, you have an additional source of public sector funding that can be accessed through local government departments. In both nations there are services for small businesses, from research and development funding through to manufacturing support. Because we're based in Wales, we've seen how local government support has helped businesses to develop new products and improve the productivity of its manufacturing facilities.

There are some differences between Innovate UK and the devolved government support programmes. The first is that, with the latter, funding isn't necessarily given as part of a competition. Instead, your bid is judged against a set of criteria based on the level of innovation you're proposing and the economic benefits your product will bring in terms of jobs and turnover. The other difference is that Innovate UK looks for ideas that are innovative at a global level, whereas devolved government schemes are usually more concerned with innovation within your own organization. These schemes change every few years, so you need to check the up-to-date requirements.

Advantages of grant funding

Grant funding is good for established businesses that have a track record and a range of products they want to add to or improve upon. And if your existing product area is relevant to an Innovate UK competition, you could be ideally placed to make a bid.

What's more, a grant gives you access to a higher level of funding than what you might receive through a crowdfunding campaign. And it's not just about the money; some grants include other support, such as expert advice and introductions to useful contacts.

Disadvantages of grant funding

You have to be eligible for grant funding, not only in terms of the nature of your business but also your product. It's not suitable, for instance, if you've had a light-bulb moment about how to solve a problem and you don't already have a business that makes and sells a range of items. It's also not for you if your product isn't technical and highly innovative.

Furthermore, while you may receive a substantial amount of funding, Innovate UK only supplies 70 percent of it and the devolved governments sometimes less. You have to find the remainder yourself.

Private investment

This is when you pitch for investment from angel investors (high net worth individuals) or investment companies. In return, you give them a share of your business. There are government schemes (such as the Seed Enterprise Investment Scheme and the Enterprise Investment Scheme, or SEIS and EIS) that offer huge tax incentives to investors when they invest in start-ups and businesses with innovative products, so the tax regime is in your favour. Many product creators aren't aware of SEIS and EIS, but they're well worth knowing about.

We've had several clients who've gained large amounts of capital from both angel investors and venture capital funds. One was a medical company that developed a diabetes product. There was a five-year development cycle involved, with huge technical challenges for delivering the project. It's hard to see how it could have been funded in any other way, and it's this kind of thing that venture capital finance is ideal for. In this company's case it was successful in raising numerous rounds of investment, and we were actively involved through the creation of prototypes, CAD models, 3D renders, and animations for presentation videos. These helped the business to capture the imagination of investors before its design went any further.

As with grant funders, both angel investors and investment houses tend not to be interested in one-person inventors. They expect to take a fair bit of risk, so they don't necessarily require a record of previous success, but they do want to be convinced of the experience and attitude within your team. A question they often ask is, 'Why are you the right people to do this?' They're buying into you as much as your product.

One venture capital organization that's worth looking into is the British Design Fund;[7] there are other similar organizations, but this has a strong presence in the UK. It's an investment house for purpose-led, British product businesses and works with them to help them grow. It not only provides investment funding but also mentoring and support, and its investors are constantly seeking new companies to buy into. If you have experience of developing products within the sectors the fund operates within, it would be worth getting in touch.

Advantages of private investment

It can transform your likelihood of success. When you have a cash injection from an investor, you'll be confident that you have enough budget to see your project through to the end. You won't have to cut corners with designs and prototypes and can invest in a high-quality end product.

Many investors aren't put off by risk, so, given that lack of finance is one of the main reasons for innovative products failing to get to market, private investment is a potential lifesaver. What's more, if your product is at all technical and risky and you're not eligible for grant funding for any reason, it's probably the only viable option for you.

---

[7] www.britishdesignfund.co.uk

Disadvantages of private investment

You have to give away a chunk of equity in exchange for the investment, so think carefully about how much you would feel comfortable parting with. It's also important to have some IP protection in place for your product. Investors are often reluctant to buy into something that's not patentable, because they'll be concerned about the ability of another business to copy your idea.

Now you know the main sources of funding, bear in mind that you don't have to choose just one option. You could start off by self-funding, and when you reach the point at which you need more money you could look at other funding strategies. In fact, it will help you to gain funding if potential investors see that you've taken on some of the risk by spending your own money to reach the prototype stage. You can never show up to an investors' meeting or a crowdfunding campaign with an idea and nothing else, so part self-funding and part external funding can be a useful combination. There's also no reason why you shouldn't apply for a combination of grants and venture capital investment; they can be complementary.

In the next chapter, we'll take the topic of finance to another level when we explore the different business models you can use to bring your product to market.

The main points

- ✓ Not having enough money is the most common reason for product ideas failing to become realities.
- ✓ Self-funding is quick and easy, but you shoulder all the risk yourself.
- ✓ Crowdfunding is open to anyone and is often successful, but you need to know how to market your idea.
- ✓ Government grants can give you a significant cash injection, but you have to be eligible to apply for one.
- ✓ Private investment is potentially open to any business with an innovative product idea, but you have to give away a percentage of your equity in exchange.

6

What's Your Business Model?

The phrase 'business model' sounds a bit technical, but all it means is the way in which you're going to deliver your product into the hands of your customers, and how they're going to pay for it. You may wonder what there is to talk about here. Surely you'll sell it to people online, or, if more appropriate, to retailers or wholesalers. That may be the best route for you, but there are other options to think about. You might be surprised at how you can increase your sales, and also the value your product has in the eyes of your customers, by being a bit more creative. You can even give your product a point of difference in its own right just through the way you sell it.

This is what's called 'business model innovation'. It's a subject that experts write whole books about so this chapter is only an overview, but the point of it is to get you thinking about how you can maximize the revenue you gain from your customers, and how you can sustain it over a longer period of time than a one-off transaction. Because while selling something once is good, selling it multiple times is even better. If you're prepared to be open-minded about how you package up your product for sale and the way in which you sell it, all sorts of exciting opportunities can emerge.

There are several types of business model:

- Direct selling
- Renting and leasing
- Razor and blade
- Subscription
- Hybrid

While you're reading about each one, ask yourself if it could be relevant to your product. What might you do differently as a result?

Direct selling

This is the most obvious and straightforward model: selling your product direct to your customers, or to a retailer or wholesaler who then sells it to consumers. It's probably the easiest way for you to get your product into the market, and for many products it's the best, but it can limit your revenue stream further down the line. Some of the reasons for that will become apparent as you explore the other business models, but one of them is down to the concept of 'planned obsolescence'.

Every product has a lifespan, and in recent years this has become increasingly short. When I was a child, my mum had a tumble dryer that seemed immortal – it must have lasted for at least 25 years. Today, manufacturers don't design products to last that long; instead, they make them so that after a certain number of uses they fail. Another factor in planned obsolescence is the effect of stylistic trends or upgrades. Your current mobile phone might work fine in terms of its hardware now, but after a number of years the software won't be supported anymore and you'll end up buying a new model. Maybe you'll even trade up so as to have the latest feature or look.

If your aim is to make a profit on your product, you need to take into account how long you want it to last. Of course, you want it to be good quality, but is there a certain lifespan you have in mind? Could you increase your sales by building in the potential for people to upgrade or renew?

Renting and leasing

This is a business model that's been around for a long time, mainly because it creates a win-win scenario for both manufacturer and consumer. Manufacturers get to sell products to people who can't afford to buy them outright, and consumers get to use products without having to invest a large sum in one go. It's worth bearing in mind that there's a subtle difference between renting and leasing. With renting you pay for the use of something and return it when you're finished, whereas with leasing you normally get to own the product after your contract is up.

In the past, renting or leasing was considered most appropriate for people on low incomes, but today the most commonly leased product is the smartphone, and it's changed how we view product ownership. Imagine if phone manufacturers had originally assessed the market opportunity for their products only on the basis of people buying them outright; they would have found their sales severely restricted. However, when smartphones first came out, we were already used to paying monthly phone bills, so we felt relatively comfortable with the idea of entering into a limited term contract to pay for the product in instalments. This not only gave phone manufacturers the chance to sell to more people but also drove their product development strategies (it's no coincidence that a new Apple or Samsung model tends to come out every year or two, and that the average contract is the same length).

This is why the rental model is becoming more widely used for high ticket items. Recently I talked to a medical company that makes CT scanners (machines that use x-rays to create computerized images of the inside of the body). They cost hundreds of thousands of pounds – so even for the health service the price is steep – and, given the highly technical nature of the product and how quickly the technology is changing, they're constantly being upgraded. This company, therefore, is planning to shift to a rental model. It makes a lot of sense, as they'll be able to get their products into the market in a way that wouldn't be possible if they were expecting all their customers to buy them outright.

Is the rental or leasing model right for my product?

Here are some questions you can ask yourself:

- Is my product prohibitively expensive for its market?
- Is it durable and re-usable so that after it's been leased by one person it can be used by another?
- Is there a reasonable level of planned obsolescence in my product that means customers will want upgrades or replacements?
- Do I have a strong enough brand reputation to enable me to gain the commitment of a contract from buyers?

Razor and blade

You know how, when you buy a razor, it comes with a handle plus a small number of blades, but as the blades need replacing you can buy them separately? That's what's called the razor and blade model; it can apply to other industries as well, but this is the most well-known application of it. The most interesting aspect is the pricing strategy. Often the manufacturer prices the handle at a non-profitable level, with the idea that, once you've bought it, you'll be happy to pay over the odds for the blades. In other words, there are two separate elements to the product, a permanent one and a consumable one, and it's the consumable one that allows the brand to generate long-term, profitable revenue.

This is similar to how the ecoegg Laundry Eggs[8] work. These are plastic, egg-shaped containers that you fill with pellets and put in your washing machine as an environmentally friendly substitute for laundry detergent. Consumers buy the egg with a starter pack of pellets, then refills at about half the price of the original; this makes the egg great value and a low barrier to switching from detergent.

More recently, some manufacturers have reversed the pricing balance of this model so that the major investment from the customer comes upfront and the consumable items are at a lower price. For instance, I have an e-ink tablet called reMarkable that I use for writing and drawing. It cost me several hundred pounds to buy, and the nibs for the pen that come with it need to be replaced over time. Given that I've committed myself both financially and usage-wise to the tablet, I'll continue buying the nibs, and in the process I'll visit the product's website on a regular basis. That allows the brand to keep maintaining my interest and attention, so when the next version of the tablet comes along, I might decide to upgrade. If it expands or diversifies its range, I could even end up purchasing another product as well.

Some manufacturers offer the consumable items on a subscription basis, thereby locking in long-term revenue. Printer brand Hewlett-Packard is a good example of this. You can buy one of its printers and purchase the ink cartridges yourself, or you can sign up

---

[8] www.ecoegg.com

for a monthly subscription to its Instant Ink service.[9] With this, as long as your printer is connected to the Internet, Hewlett-Packard knows how much you're printing and sends you replacement cartridges when needed. This makes life more convenient for you as a user, and for Hewlett-Packard it locks you in as a long-term customer and prevents you defecting to other cartridge brands.

Is the razor and blade model right for my product?

Here are some questions you can ask yourself:

- Can my product be divided into permanent and consumable elements?
- Do I have IP in my product so that competitors can't mimic the consumable items, thereby taking away my opportunity for long-term revenue?
- Do I have a marketing system to keep in touch with people who've bought my permanent product so that I can sell consumable items to them?
- Do I have other products in my range that I could use my marketing system to sell?

Subscription

As you can see from the Hewlett-Packard example above, when there's an opportunity to sell consumable

---

[9] https://instantink.hpconnected.com

items that work with a permanent one, there's often the chance to lock in customer loyalty by setting up a subscription. However, the subscription model can also be a way of selling a whole product in its own right. It works best for relatively low-value items, as these examples show.

Bristle[10] sells environmentally friendly bamboo toothbrushes, along with accessories such as biodegradable toothpaste and floss. Customers buy the toothbrush, then subscribe on a regular basis for new ones, returning their used brush for recycling if they wish. The benefit to Bristle is that it has loyal customers who stay with it for the long term. The benefit to customers is that they're encouraged to renew their brush more regularly than they normally would, which means that their teeth are cleaner. Also, they don't have to remember to buy a new brush.

Another example is Splosh,[11] which sells household soaps and detergents such as bathroom and kitchen cleaning products and shower gels. Customers buy the container bottles and subscribe to (or buy ad hoc) the consumable items as packets of concentrate, which they add to the bottles and mix with water. This reduces the environmental impact of transporting heavy liquids, and the fact that the bottles are re-usable adds to the attraction. The benefit to Splosh is that they gain regular revenue from reliable customers, and the benefit to their customers is that they have an easy way of helping the environment.

---

[10] https://wearebristle.com

[11] www.splosh.com

Subscription isn't right for every product, but for some it can make a lot of sense. Dollar Shave Club,[12] for instance, sells subscriptions for razor blades and, two years after launch, was sold for $1 billion. The main reason for its huge valuation was its captive audience, which allowed it to sell a range of men's grooming products in addition to its razors and blades. This shows how building a community and keeping it loyal can be even more valuable than the profit you make from the original product itself.

However, there's a sustainability question to be answered if you decide to set up a subscription business because it's important not to encourage waste. Brands that have done well with it are often those, such as Bristle and Splosh, that offer an environmentally friendly product or sell items that genuinely need replacing. If you're selling replacement items for the sake of it without considering the environmental impact, it may be time to reconsider.

Is the subscription model right for my product?

Here are some questions you can ask yourself:

- Is my product relatively low cost?
- Does it need regularly replacing?
- Are there related products that I could sell as well?
- Do I have the marketing capability to build a loyal audience?
- Is my product environmentally sustainable?

---

[12] https://uk.dollarshaveclub.com

Hybrid

The final business model is a hybrid one in which you combine one or more of the above. There's an almost infinite number of ways you could do this, but one is to sell your product and have a free app that goes with it. A good example is an ECG (electrocardiogram) monitor called AliveCor.[13] It consists of a physical unit upon which people can place their fingertips, with an accompanying free smartphone app that reads the results. Once you've bought the product you can use it as often as you like at no additional cost, but you can also pay for feedback from medical professionals via the app. In this way the brand makes money in two ways: by selling the units and by upselling additional services through its app.

Another example is Philips Hue light bulbs.[14] These are bulbs that contain a computer chip that communicates with a free app on your smartphone or smart assistant. This allows you to control your lights from wherever you happen to be (even if you're not in the house) and also to create special lighting effects. Through this business model innovation, Philips has given its brand a strong point of difference.

You could also consider making and delivering your product in a way that's different to your competitors. Opendesk[15] is an online platform that allows people to download designer furniture templates for free and pay for the items to be manufactured. The company sends the templates to one of its profession-

---

[13] www.alivecor.co.uk
[14] www.philips-hue.com/en-gb/products/smart-light-bulbs
[15] www.opendesk.cc

al makers, which crafts them locally to the customer and ships direct. Opendesk makes money by charging a percentage commission on the making costs, and designers receive royalties for their designs.

Alternatively, could your product give added value to your customers if they bought more than one of it? A friend of mine, Paul, told me recently that his family has four Alexas. 'Why do you need four?' I asked. He replied that it was so they could use them to speak to each other in different rooms, much like an intercom. This got me thinking about the potential for multiple items of a product to be used in a way that makes them more than the sum of their parts. For instance, think of TVs, which many people have more than one of so they can use them in different rooms of the house. Could you develop your product in such a way that it creates demand for multiple ownership?

You could also generate additional revenue by selling accessories for your product. Think back to the Bluetooth speaker example in Chapter 3. In order to save costs, we decided not to include a belt clip for the speaker, but we could sell it as an additional item. That would have the dual benefit of keeping core costs down and making extra sales as well.

Is a hybrid model right for your product?

Here are some questions you can ask yourself:

- Does my product require an app for it to work? Are there ways in which I can use this to generate extra revenue?

- Is there an inbuilt advantage, for both me and my customers, to giving away all or part of my product for free?
- Is there another potential customer for my product – such as an organization that might buy the data generated by it – that would make giving it away for free worthwhile?
- Is there an innovative way in which I can produce my product, making it cheaper, easier, or more sustainable for me and my customers?
- Would my product offer extra value if people bought more than one of it?
- Are there accessories I could sell in addition to my main product?

Where to go from here

I've given you a lot to think about and I hope you feel inspired by the endless possibilities of business model innovation – you can do a lot of exciting things with your product by selling it in different ways. However, bear in mind that it's not a good idea to force your product into a model – decide what you want to make first and then work out which route to market is best. You also need to understand your target customer well enough to judge what they would value about your business model, rather than assuming what they want.

A useful tool to help you brainstorm the options is the Business Model Canvas. Originally created by Alexander Osterwalder, a Swiss business theorist and entrepreneur, it's a simple, one-page planning aid that will help you to map out the various elements of your product business, and you can download it from various sources online.[16] It prompts you to think about your product's unique selling point, your customers, your route to market, and many other areas, some of which we've explored in this book.

In the next chapter we'll dive into one of my favourite topics – manufacturing strategy.

The main points

✓ There are many more ways to deliver your product into your customers' hands than direct sales.

✓ If your product (and customer) is suitable for a different model, you can increase your long-term revenue by exploring alternative options.

✓ These include renting and leasing, razor and blade, subscription, and hybrid business models.

✓ Remember that the model should be in service of the product rather than the other way around.

---

[16] Here's one: https://en.wikipedia.org/wiki/Business_ Model_Canvas

7

Your Manufacturing Strategy

'How much will it cost to make my product? I'm not sure how many units I should budget for.'

'Where will I get my product produced? I've heard that China is the cheapest place, but I'm worried about quality.'

'How is a manufacturer going to take my designs and turn them into a finished item? What's the process?'

It's natural to be full of questions about how your product will be made. Having a set of beautiful designs is part of the journey, but until those designs are translated into an equally beautiful and functional finished article you only have a product in theory, not practice.

This chapter walks you through the decisions you need to make about where and how your product will be manufactured. You'll discover what factors to take into account when working out your costs, how to decide on your country of manufacture, and the top-line processes involved. By the end, you'll be able to talk about tooling, supply chains, and the relative pros and cons of factories in China and the UK. These are all things you need to know if your product is to be a profitable success.

How much will my product cost to make?

We touched on manufacturing costs in Chapter 5 when we talked about funding, but we'll explore it in more detail here. It's an important area because your manufacturing costs will almost certainly dwarf your design costs. There are lots of decisions for you to get right if you're to end up with something that not only gives you a return on investment but is also the right quality for your market.

There are several factors to take into account when it comes to cost:

- The country your factory is located in
- The order quantity you commit to
- The type of tooling you choose
- Material availability and currency fluctuations

The country your factory is located in

Most people tend to assume that their product will be produced in China. That may well be the best choice for you, but it's important not to overlook the UK, as there are many benefits to making a product here as well. I'll go into the various differences between Chinese and UK manufacturing later on, but let's focus on costs for now.

If your product needs a high level of manual input for assembly, it probably makes sense to produce it in China because the labour cost is lower. The average Chinese factory worker earns around £3 an hour; if you compare that to the minimum wage in the UK, you can appreciate the difference. Even if the assembly only involves a simple operation, multiply that by 10,000 and it's not hard to see how that can bump up your production costs. If, however, your product involves little or no assembly, it might be more cost-effective to make it in the UK – especially when you take into account the saving you'll make on shipping costs.

That isn't to say that the UK is always the most expensive place to manufacture high-assembly products. For large enough volumes it can be viable to assemble products here using robots. For instance, I know a company that makes huge quantities of plastic kitchen products, such as bins and plate drainers; some of these items have parts that need to be put together and are being manufactured in the UK using robot technology.

The order quantity you commit to

All factories, no matter where they're located, base their price on how many units you order. As you'd expect, if you want to manufacture 50,000 units, you'll receive a better deal than if you go for 10,000. Not only that, but factories have their own cut-off points under which they won't even consider an order – this is what they call their minimum order quantity (often referred to as an MOQ). This tends to be lower in the UK than in China; a UK factory might agree to a minimum order quantity of 2,000 units, for instance, whereas a Chinese one would only entertain the idea of producing at least 10,000.

It's important to start thinking early on about what order volume makes sense for you, not only in terms of the initial order but also how many items you're likely to sell over the first year or two. If you feel confident that you'll sell 30,000 in the first year, you'll have a much more profitable product than if you go for a more conservative estimate of 5,000.

The type of tooling you choose

I'll explain more about what tooling is later on, but for now you can think of it as being the mould or template that the factory will make in order to churn out multiple copies of your product. It's a fixed, one-off cost that you pay at the beginning of the manufacturing process, and it can be more expensive than you think. There are three main types of tooling material – polyurethane, aluminium, and steel – and they each involve a different level of investment.

Polyurethane: with this, a mould is made of flexible polyurethane, liquid plastic is poured inside, and it's set with heat under a vacuum. The mould is peeled away and the finished plastic part is released. The advantage of polyurethane is that it's low cost; you might pay only £2,000–£3,000 for a mould. However, it's labour intensive to detach the mould from each part, and the mould only lasts for around 15 units before it has to be replaced. It's therefore most suitable for low order volumes such as prototypes or pieces of highly specialized equipment that you're only going to sell a handful of.

Aluminium or steel: with these, the mould is made of metal, which lasts a lot longer than polyurethane; it's possible to get many thousands of units out of it before it wears out. The difference between aluminium and steel is in the relative longevity they offer, with a corresponding difference in price. While an aluminium tool might give you 10,000 units before it's replaced and cost in the region of £20,000, a steel one could last for 500,000 but cost in the region of £50,000. Of course, these costs are only approximate, as they depend on the number and complexity of the parts for the product assembly.

Your choice of tooling material is therefore down to how many items you think you'll sell. If yours is an innovative product and you're not sure how many people will buy it, why spend all that money on a steel tool? An aluminium one will have a shorter lifespan, and if your product takes off, you'll have enough revenue and confidence to invest in a steel tool then. It's worth thinking strategically about how much you invest in tooling, and when.

Material availability and currency fluctuations

These are out of your control, but it's still important to know about them. When you order from a factory in China (or anywhere outside of the UK), changes in the exchange rate have a direct impact on your unit cost. Shipping costs can also go up and down, and together these factors make it difficult to predict your costs with certainty. In addition, there can be times when certain raw materials are in short supply, and this will affect their price no matter where in the world your manufacturer is located. For instance, during the Covid-19 pandemic, reduced production output caused a polymer shortage and also a lack of silicon for electronic chips.

'Okay', you might be thinking. 'It's good to know about these cost factors, but they don't help me to estimate how much my product will cost to make. I need to understand that so I can budget and decide on a retail price. How do I do that?'

The answer is: 'With difficulty.' Of course, you want to know whether you'll receive a high enough return on your investment to make it worth going ahead with your product – that's understandable. But until it has been fully designed, you won't be able to gain a detailed cost breakdown from your manufacturer. It's like pricing a holiday when you don't know where you want to go. So while gaining a feel for your production costs at an early stage of your journey is valuable, it's also challenging to do with any accuracy.

There are, however, a couple of benchmarks you can use as a guide. One is to see if there's a similar product to yours already on the market; if there is, you can make the reasonable assumption that the cost of production is 30 to 40 percent of the selling price. Naturally there will be factors you don't know about, such as how many units of it were produced, but it gives you a steer. Another is to talk to your designer. If they've been working in the industry for a while, they may have enough experience to give an educated guess based on the number of parts within the product and the complexity of the tooling. It's only a rough guide, but it's better than nothing.

China versus the UK

As you've seen, there are usually cost advantages to manufacturing in China as opposed to the UK. What's more, although quality used to be more questionable in China, it has improved in recent years. It's now just as good a place as any from a quality perspective, and any variability isn't so much to do with the country as with which factory was involved.

This might make China seem like a no-brainer for you, but there are also advantages to the UK. Not only do you not have high shipping costs and unpredictable currency fluctuations to contend with, you can also work with a local supplier who is easy to communicate with.

Here are some of the factors, other than cost, to think about when deciding where to manufacture your product.

Your market location

You can save a significant amount on shipping and transportation if you manufacture your product in the same country in which you plan to sell it. Brexit and Covid-19 have played havoc with the shipping network both in terms of cost and reliability, and this has made manufacturing locally more attractive. So if you're aiming to sell only in the UK, it might make sense to base your production here. The same goes if your main market is in a specific territory abroad; we recently worked with one client who was making a product for the US, which was why they decided to manufacture it there.

Ease of communication

Do you like the idea of being able to jump in the car and visit your factory if there's a problem? Would you love to see your product coming off the production line? From a communication perspective there's an inbuilt advantage to manufacturing in the UK, and it can be worth a lot.

Obviously you can't do this with a Chinese factory, although you can work with one of several UK-based agents who liaise with factories in China. You give them your design and they identify who could best make it, as well as costing it for you and placing the order with the factory. They also manage the shipping, which can be extremely helpful when it comes to combining your order with others, as you can save a lot of money that way. In addition, an agent gives you more leverage with a factory than you could achieve on your own. You pay an extra 10 to 15 percent, but it can be worth it.

Availability of machinery and materials

There have been times when we've not been able to find a UK factory that carries out a particular process or can achieve a specific finish and have had to look further afield to get the result we want. In China, however, you'll find a greater range of equipment and manufacturing technologies. There are also materials that are only available in certain parts of the world. Neodymium is a rare metal that is used in vast numbers of consumer products, such as in your mobile phone to create the vibration alert; it's used because a tiny amount gives out a strong magnetic field. It's almost exclusively mined in China, which is one of the reasons why phone brands choose to manufacture there.

How much certainty you want

Cost used to be the only main factor that product owners considered when deciding where to base their manufacturing, which led them to choose China most of the time. That's still true to a certain extent, but brands are now coming to realize that manufacturing there can expose them to risks such as transport delays and political interference. We saw this first-hand during the early months of the Covid-19 pandemic, when we helped various UK factories to rapidly design new production lines for protective equipment such as visors and gowns. These products had previously been made in China but were slow to get here and weren't arriving in high enough volumes. The shift towards bringing manufacturing back home is often called 're-shoring'.

There's another aspect to certainty, which is having control over your product's sales. If you manufacture in China, you can't be sure that the factory isn't making extra units and selling them themselves locally. I once spoke to a designer who saw a chopping board he'd designed for sale on eBay and Alibaba; it was exactly the same as his and had obviously been made from his tooling without his permission. We've not experienced this issue ourselves because we work through agents that have relationships with reliable Chinese factories. However, I've never heard of it happening at all in UK factories.

What you need to know: tooling

You may be unsure about what tooling is. It's the first step in the production process, and its purpose is to create the various parts that will be assembled to make the finished product. The most common type of tool is one designed for injection moulding. Here, pellets of melted plastic are fed into a mould, the liquid material is cooled until it solidifies, the tool opens, and the part pops out. Your manufacturer will use your designer's 3D CAD model to create a unique tool for your product that fits inside their injection moulding machine. This is similar in some ways to baking a cake. You pour the batter into the tin, heat it up in the oven, and leave it there for exactly the right amount of time to ensure that it's cooked through.

If you open the door too soon it will sink, and if you leave it for too long it will crack. Of course, while the cake analogy helps to illustrate the process, in reality it's far more complicated than that. Creating a tool from a 3D CAD model is a highly complex procedure, and one that takes time to get right.

Something you need to be aware of is that although you pay for your product's tool, you don't necessarily own it. Chinese factories usually quote two prices for tooling: a higher one that allows you to own it and a lower one that enables them to. Why would you want to own your tool? This story is a good example. We worked with a company that manufactured all its products in China. The business wanted to move its production to the UK because of exorbitant shipping costs, but it didn't own its tooling. Even if it had, a tool made for one injection mould machine wouldn't necessarily work in another, so moving it was always going to be a risk. The company was stuck between a rock and a hard place: re-tooling its product range at tremendous cost, or carrying on paying the cost of shipping and struggling to remain profitable.

There's not much you can do about this, but you do need to know about it because the decisions that you make now about your tooling can have repercussions further down the line. At the very least it's a good idea to understand why a tooling quote from a Chinese factory might be much cheaper than from a UK one; it's not just about labour costs but also about who owns the tool.

What you need to know: supply chains

Suppose you want to make an at-home heart monitor with a plastic casing and a printed circuit board (PCB) inside, as well as a cloth storage bag. It would be perfect if you could find one factory to produce all the items, but this is rarely possible. In China there are manufacturers that specialize in certain types of whole products, such as torches, but if your product is at all innovative or unusual, you'll almost certainly need to have the parts made in a variety of places. The problem is, who will co-ordinate the various different elements? Unfortunately, it can be hard to find one place to take responsibility. Normally the factory that creates the PCBs sends them to the one that handles the plastics moulding, and the latter assembles the product. Given that the electronics are the most valuable part, however, they might not want to do that.

We experienced this recently when we tried to have a product made in Korea. We found a factory that produced good-quality, plastic moulded products at a great price, but we couldn't find a facility in the same country to make the PCBs cost effectively. We looked at producing the PCBs in the UK, but that would have meant sending them to Korea for assembly with the plastic parts, only for Korea to ship the finished product back here. The other option was for Korea to send the plastic parts here, but we couldn't find anyone to handle the assembly in the UK. In the end, our client decided to use a Chinese manufacturer who handled the whole job, making the supply chain easier to manage.

This is where Chinese agents come into their own. Your product might need the involvement of as many as four or five manufacturers. Co-ordinating this yourself, with lead times and minimum order quantities to juggle, would be almost impossible – far better to leave it to an agent who knows what they're doing.

In the next chapter we'll look at where you plan to sell your product and through what channels. It's the final step in its journey into the world.

The main points

✓ It's important to start thinking early about how much your product will cost to make.

✓ Unit costs depend on various factors: the location of the factory, the minimum order quantity, the type of tooling, the exchange rate, and shipping costs.

✓ Don't automatically assume that China is the best place to make your product – the UK has various inbuilt advantages and may be a better option for you.

✓ Consider how you're going to co-ordinate the various elements of your manufacturing supply chain.

8

Your Go-To-Market Strategy

Have you ever seen a product in a shop or on a website and wondered why the brand that owned it decided to put it there? Why that particular store or that specific website? Why not somewhere else? It's the sort of thing that we tend to take for granted, but when it's your product, you're the one who has to decide how and where it's made available for purchase. This is another way of describing your go-to-market strategy.

There are five main routes to market:

- License your product
- Sell online
- Sell to retail stores
- Use a distributor or reseller
- Sell to the public sector

If you already have a business selling products and you're happy with the channels you use, this chapter won't be relevant to you. But if you've never sold a product before, it will help you to decide which path is right for you and your product.

License your product

If you're like many of the clients we work with, you might be planning to license your product to a branded manufacturer or retailer. The idea is that you hand over your designs to them, they manufacture and sell the product, then they pay you a royalty for every unit sold. I can understand why it's an appealing option; if designing your product is the part of the process that you find most exciting, why not pass the baton to another party from that point on? You don't have to be involved with manufacturing and marketing and their associated costs and risks. Instead, you get the satisfaction of seeing your product on the shelf without having to do anything to put it there.

However, while I don't want to puncture your enthusiasm, the likelihood of you being able to strike a licensing deal is slim. In fact, even though some of our clients have got as far as having formal conversations with potential licensees, they've never managed to sign a contract with them. I'm not saying that it's impossible, but in my experience it's rare.

The main reason for this is the commercial viability of your product. We worked with a business that invented a device designed to make measuring and fitting floors easier for wooden flooring contractors. To us, it seemed like a product that solved a genuine problem, and the company's research confirmed this. We created a working prototype from high quality materials that looked and felt like the finished item, and Simon, the business owner, managed to secure meetings with some large DIY retailers to discuss a licensing deal. But while the retailers agreed that it was a great product, they weren't convinced that it had enough sales potential. In other words, the rejection was nothing to do with the product itself, but the low likelihood of the retailers making a return on their investment. You have to realize that a licensee isn't interested in a few sales here and there – it wants to generate serious revenue for it to be worth its while to make and sell someone else's design.

Despite this, maybe you're determined to go ahead with a licensing route to market. If so, these are the things to be aware of so that you maximize your chances of signing up to a deal that works for you.

Who pays for what?

Formalizing a licensing deal is more complex than simply handing over your design and walking away. Some licensees might prefer you to do this, but others may insist that you pay for certain elements of the manufacture and marketing. I spoke with someone recently who invented a special type of bicycle seat. He did manage to reach an agreement with a licensee, but the licensee insisted that he pay for the tooling himself, as it wanted to minimize the financial risk.

When will you be paid?

The payment schedule is important. Will you receive your royalties every year? Every quarter? Every month? And does your contract have an end point, after which you'll receive nothing?

Is sales volume a factor?

Will you receive a higher or lower percentage according to how many products the licensee sells? And will it only pay you after a certain threshold has been reached? Trigger points are important to agree on upfront because it's possible that a brand could take your design and then do nothing with it; it might just want to stop a competitor having the product, for instance.

Exclusivity options

If you do manage to obtain a licensing deal, is it best to have it with just one company? Would the terms of the deal preclude you from also making and selling the product yourself? And what about licensing to multiple licensees, perhaps abroad or in different markets? This all depends on your product and who it appeals to.

Intellectual property protection

As we discussed in Chapter 4 when exploring the benefits of patents versus design registration, a well-known brand is unlikely to give a licensing deal to somebody who has no serious IP in their product. Unless you think your product can sell on the basis of brand differentiation alone (as it might if it was a clothing product, for instance), a patent is a must and your IP protection must be watertight.

Liability

If your product were to fail or cause an injury to someone who bought it, who would be responsible? You or the licensee? The licensee may want to protect itself against any future claims, so, before the market launch, it's important to discuss where the liability lies.

In summary, while licensing might seem like the most hassle-free way to get your product into the market, there are many things to think about if you land a deal. Not only will you have to negotiate with a major business to ensure that you receive a fair offer, you'll also only make a small percentage on each sale. If your licensee is a well-known brand or retailer, it's likely to sell more products more quickly than you could, but the royalties won't come anywhere near the amount you'd earn if you kept ownership of it.

Sell online

Fifteen or twenty years ago, approaching high street retailers was the most obvious route to market for most products, but now it's setting up a website and selling online. Not only is this how many people choose to buy, but it's also much easier to design a commercial website than it ever was before. And while you have to pay the upfront costs yourself, you can generate immediate sales and receive the full amount of revenue into your own pocket. You also have visibility of your sales in real time and the satisfaction of nurturing your product all the way from the original concept to getting it into the hands of your customers.

It's no wonder that many of our clients choose to take this path. One example is the business that owns the Lift Buddy, an innovative gadget that makes it easier for tradespeople to lift and carry heavy fire doors when installing them. The company runs Facebook ads to drive people to its website, and, while it's a niche item and so doesn't sell in high numbers, the site receives a steady stream of traffic. Another example is the air-quality monitor that we looked at in Chapter 2. The company ran a successful Kickstarter campaign to raise funding, then used the interest generated by that to drive traffic to its website. This enabled it to build a community around the brand, with consumers often returning to the site even after they'd bought the product. This shows how having your own website can give you a long-term platform for sales, with the option of adding accessories or even other products to your range as time goes by.

The downside of selling through your own website is that it can be slow to scale your sales because building web traffic takes time. Then, when people do arrive at the site, they may feel unsure about buying from an unknown brand. However, if you have a good understanding of online advertising, you can get around this by running campaigns to drive people to your website. Not only can they deliver the numbers you need, but they also create awareness and familiarity ('It's all over Instagram and Facebook so it must be okay'). Social proof is also important when building an online presence, and you can gain this by leveraging the power of influencers and making the most of the reviews you get. These all add to your credibility.

It's worth bearing in mind that social media advertising works best if your product solves a problem that people are unlikely to know they have, or that they assume there's no solution for. That's because it captures people's attention while they're looking for other things, such as news about their friends. The Lift Buddy is a good example of that. Many fire door installers wouldn't know that there's an easier way of doing their jobs and so wouldn't be searching for a solution, but they might see a Facebook ad as they are scrolling through their feeds. Search engine ads, in contrast, work best if people are actively searching for a solution to their problem.

If you don't want to set up your own website and drive traffic to it, you can trade through online marketplaces such as Amazon, eBay, and Etsy. Not only do they display your product to their pre-existing audience of buyers, they also build trust through their customer reviews. They are, however, more expensive to work with, as they take a cut of your revenue; as a result, they're probably not a long-term option if you want to build a profitable business. I wouldn't advise making them your only sales channel.

Sell to retail stores

Have you, at any stage of your product journey, imagined what it would be like to go to a store and see it on the shelf? Have you thought about that selfie you'll take of yourself standing next to it? If you have, you're not alone. It's a proud moment when you finally get to witness the fruits of your labour in 'real life'.

That's one reason for wanting to sell your product in a retail store. Another is that you might believe it's where you'll achieve the best sales volumes, especially if you manage to get it into a large chain. The rationale is that, when shoppers browse the shelves, they'll pick up your product as an impulse buy or because it offers a solution that they didn't know existed.

While I can't comment on the subjective satisfaction of seeing your product on the shelf, I do need to manage your expectations about sales. We worked with a company to design a children's toy that Ranjit, the product owner, sold into a prestigious retailer with a 50-store chain. This was no mean feat, as large store groups reject far more proposals than they accept. You might think that the retailer would sell impressive numbers of the toy, but in fact it only shifts around one per store per week. When you consider the amount of effort that goes into getting a product listed by a retailer, it's not a brilliant return on investment. Where Ranjit has found the listing to be more worthwhile, though, is in the cachet it's given his brand. He saw an immediate uptick in sales from his own website when it went into the stores because some people saw the toy on the shelves and decided to buy it from him. Also, being stocked there has given him leverage when selling it into other chains.

As I mentioned, it's not easy to get your product into stores – retail buyers are notoriously reluctant to meet with product owners, mainly because they're approached by so many. There's an alternative to this, however, which is to list your product on an online marketplace for retail buyers. There are a few available, such as RangeMe.[17] Buyers can browse the site, and, if they see a product they're interested in, they can contact the owner to start a conversation.

If selling into retail stores is something you want to do, it's worth knowing about some of the issues you may have to deal with.

Trial quantities

A retailer may initially agree to stock your product but only up to a limited number of units, or only in selected outlets. It may also insist on buying your product on a sale or return basis, in which case if it doesn't sell you have to refund the cost of the products.

Margins

Buyers at large retailers are aggressive negotiators and will insist on the lowest price they can. This will reduce your margin, which means that retail will not be as profitable as selling direct to consumers from your own website.

Packaging

You might find that a retailer will want you to change your packaging. This could be so that it works with their fixtures and fittings, or because they don't

---

[17] www.rangeme.com

think your current version promotes the product well enough. You certainly won't be able to get away with just presenting a product to them – they'll also want to see what goes around it.

Just as with licensing, retail isn't the silver bullet that many people think it is when it comes to getting a product to market. It takes a lot of time and energy, and you don't have control over the end result. Yes, it can be exciting to see your product on a shelf, but ask yourself if that's really why you created your product in the first place. It's also worth exploring whether you can combine retail with selling via your own website, or with a distributor (which we'll go into below).

Use a distributor or reseller

Suppose you want to sell your product abroad. Where would you start? Find out what retailers exist over there and contact them direct? Fly over and try to meet with them? It sounds pretty complicated, but the alternative is to work with a distributor. Their job is to be the intermediary between you and the retailers, as they have a product portfolio that they sell into retail outlets on your behalf.

Obviously there's an additional cost to using a reseller distribution network, but it does allow you to enter new territories and sell into new stores. A good distributor will have 'on the ground' knowledge and access to an established network of stores, so it's a relatively quick and easy way of expanding internationally.

We had a client, Sarah, who saw that she was making sales from the US on her UK-based website.

That led her to explore expanding into the US market, so she identified some distributors that were sector-specific and had built relationships with the kinds of retailers that would stock her product. This allowed her to sell to shops that she would never have known about, let alone be able to deal with, on her own.

I don't see many product owners exploring distribution as a route to international markets. However, this route seems like a valid one when you consider the volumes that you might be able to shift if you use one.

Sell to the public sector

The public sector works a bit differently from other routes to market, in that it operates through tenders and also through its own supply chain. Suppose a new school or hospital is being built; the local authority or trust will put out a tender asking for businesses to bid to supply certain products. If you're successful you'll be put in their catalogue, which means that the school or hospital can buy direct from you. The NHS is more complex, in that not only does it operate tenders as above, but it also has its own supply chain that acts like a purchasing department. It buys up stock and holds it within the supply chain, and hospital trusts can purchase products from that stock.

If you want to sell your product into the public sector, you need to understand what systems and processes are involved. Whether it be responding to tenders or selling to purchasing departments, there are established systems that you have to work with if you're to get it in front of the right people.

Looking at these five routes to market, it won't have escaped your notice that they're not all mutually exclusive. For instance, you can sell to retailers and on your own website, and you can sell to the public sector as well as to retailers. In fact, it's important to be in as many places as possible, not only to maximize your sales but also to build brand awareness. Naturally this will depend on what kind of product you have, but don't think of it as being viable for only one route or another.

If you're finding it hard to decide what to do, you can go back to your 'why'. What's the primary reason you wanted to design a product in the first place? Was it to create a business that you can make money from, to have the satisfaction of seeing your creation out in the world, or something else? Whichever route you choose, it's important that it satisfies your needs as a product creator.

In the next chapter we'll go through the entire design process so that you can see how products are taken from concept to working prototype.

The main points

- ✓ There are several ways of getting your product into the marketplace so that people can buy it.
- ✓ Licensing may appear attractive, but it rarely happens in practice.

✓ Online selling is the most common way to sell a new product because it offers control over the selling process and high profit margins.

✓ Retail can be a viable route, but it's difficult to get a product accepted and you're unlikely to sell as many units as you might think.

✓ Distributors are invaluable if you want to sell your product abroad.

✓ The public sector has its own requirements and processes when it comes to buying products for its users.

✓ Consider your 'why' when deciding what route to take.

9

How Your Product Is Designed

You've learned a lot about the business aspects of putting a product into the market – knowledge that will help you to create something that solves a genuine problem, makes you money, and gives you the satisfaction you're looking for. But what happens when you approach a design consultancy with your idea? How do the thoughts in your head get translated into a physical item that both looks good and does what it's supposed to? Here's where I go through the stages of the design process so that you're prepared for what's to come.

At ITERATE, just like at most product design consultancies, we have a system that we've developed. It's based on what's called the Rapid Product Development Pathway, because the more quickly you get your product to market, the stronger your competitive advantage. Naturally our own process is the one I know the best, but you'll find variations in other consultancies.

Before we get into it, it's worth pointing out that some stages take longer than others. It partly depends on what kind of product you're creating; the certification phase for a medical-grade testing kit, for instance, might take longer than for a simple consumer item. Also, you may not necessarily enter the process at the beginning. If you're an established business experienced in product design, you might arrive at an agency having already completed the first stage; if you've never done it before, you're likely to start at phase one.

1. Foresight

As we've explored already, there are certain problems that, if you don't solve at the beginning of a project, can come back to bite you later. They slow down the development or, in some cases, prevent a product from reaching the market at all. Given that our philosophy is to create products as rapidly as possible, anything we can do to minimize the likelihood of that happening is worth our attention. Our aim in this phase is therefore to identify the technical and commercial challenges as early as possible, and to address them before they become showstoppers.

There are three main areas that we focus on:

- Intellectual property
- Market need and target audience
- Technical feasibility and safety standards

Intellectual property

Some product ideas trigger a 'red flag' with us when it comes to IP protection. It might be that there are competitor products in the market already with IP attached to them that you need to be careful not to infringe. Or it could be that a significant part of your strategy is to create something patentable. Either way, we'd ask a patent attorney to carry out a preliminary search before we come up with any design concepts. If we were to start designing before we knew what the IP landscape looked like, we might have to go back to the drawing board later on, and this would have cost and time implications.

Market need and target audience

If you haven't already nailed the problem that your product is solving or been specific about the market it's aimed at, we help you to resolve this now. As we discussed in Chapters 2 and 3, it's crucial to understand whether people will want to buy your product and who those people are. If we were to go ahead with concepts that were based only on assumptions, we'd run the risk of designing something that wouldn't sell.

Technical feasibility and safety standards

Some product ideas are fantastic in theory but not possible to create in real life – or not in a commercially viable way – and adjustments need to be made. There's often a trade-off between making what's ideally wanted and what's possible within the confines of the technology that exists to deliver it. A common issue is size; the more capabilities a product has, the larger the item usually has to be. That might be fine if it doesn't need to be portable or compact, but many products are intended to be worn or carried around.

A good example is the design we created for a wrist-worn location tracking device, which I talked about in Chapter 2. Our client originally wanted to include a number of different technologies within it, such as GPS and voice activation; in addition, they ideally wanted it to have a battery that lasted for a month. We scoped out their requirements during the Foresight phase, but discovered that including all those features would make the product prohibitively expensive to buy. What's more, it wasn't possible to have such a powerful battery that would also be light enough to wear on the wrist. In the end, we reduced the number of functions and the battery size, and our client ended up with a sleek and functional product that delivered what it really needed to.

Safety standards are related to technical feasibility, in that some products are safety critical and have to comply with certain regulations. If we don't know what those are from the beginning, we could find ourselves having to carry out extensive redesigns later on. I'll cover this area more fully in the Certify step.

You can see how IP, market need, technical feasibility, and safety standards are important areas to cover before you go ahead with the design concepts. If your designer goes shooting off in the wrong direction, it can create a lot of rework further down the line. We consider the Foresight part of the process to be so essential that we sometimes do it as a separate piece of work, just to see if a product idea is technically and commercially feasible. After that, we can all be confident in going forward.

2. Concept

In many ways this is my favourite phase because it's the most creative. To start off, we normally create two kinds of mood board. The first shows competitor products or, if there are no direct competitors, products that already exist in that space. We want to gain a feel for what users in the target market value and what the product would need to look like if it was to appeal to them. The second kind of board focuses on what we call linear markets: those that run alongside the market for the product we're designing. If we were creating a domestic product, for instance, we might look at heavy industry to discover whether there are some aspects of the mechanical design that we can transfer to ours. This cross-fertilization between sectors can be a rich source of inspiration.

The next step is to sketch out a handful of concepts, each embodying a different route forward. They're pretty raw, but at the same time detailed enough to take into account how the product will work and what it looks like. We consider how many parts it might be made from, how those parts would be fitted together, and what internal components will be required. This goes back to the technical feasibility I mentioned above. If we were to underestimate the space needed inside the product for electronics, we'd end up with something twice as large as originally intended. Whereas if we know how it should work internally, we can take account of that when creating the aesthetics.

For our client this is the first time that they've seen a visual representation of what, until then, they've only had in their mind's eye. It's an exciting moment, although it can be a surprise for them to see solutions that look different to what they imagined. It's important to explore the options, though, as there will be pros and cons to each. One concept, for instance, could appeal to an important market segment, but another would be easier to manufacture and therefore cheaper to produce, or another may have environmental benefits.

Sometimes it's the functionality of a concept that provokes debate, and sometimes it's the way it looks. An example of the former is a device we designed to detect sounds that are inaudible to the human ear, such as those produced by wind turbines and pylons. These sounds can cause health problems such as tinnitus and migraines, so our client wanted to create something to neutralize the noise. The thinking was that the user would plug a matchbox-sized gadget into their mobile phone and control it via an app. We felt it was important that it didn't impede the portability of the phone, so we came up with various options, including a clip on the back with an extending jack. Our client, however, preferred a more conservative concept that sat below the phone.

For another client we created concepts for a sensor that monitored the water level in cat bowls and automatically topped it up. Some of the options were quite futuristic and some were more traditional; each would have appealed to a different market, and the client chose to go for the traditional one. This shows how considering the market is a critical factor in choosing the aesthetics of a design, and why knowing who you're aiming at is so important when it comes to making the right decision.

3. Development

Once our client has picked a design concept they want to take forward, or alternatively two or three they want to combine, we move into the Development phase. This is when we firm up what the final concept will be. It's not always required – if everyone is enthusiastic about one of the initial options, there may be no need to look at more – but there's usually some refinement needed.

4. Detail

In this phase, we create 3D CAD models of the finalized concept. It's a stage when having an eye on how the product will be manufactured becomes increasingly important. We need to envisage how strong the parts should be, what materials they'll be made out of, and how they're going to fit together. If we envisage that a product will be moulded from plastic, for instance, then the design will be different to one made out of wood or even a different type of moulding process. If we don't take all this into account at the Detail stage, we could create a lot of rework at the point when we hand over to the manufacturer.

In the process, we often do some rudimentary prototyping. If we're creating a piece of technology for users to wear on their bodies, for instance, then the fit would be important. So we might create some quick 3D prints from our CAD model to enable us to do fit testing, which allows us to refine the design.

When developing technology products, it's important to think from the inside out, with the internals driving the design of the externals. That's because this type of product usually contains a number of printed circuit boards, the size of which dictate the capacity of the outer housing. It's relatively easy to create something that looks great on the outside, but if we don't make sure that it can hold everything it needs to, we'll end up with a product that's several times larger than everyone envisaged – which can be messy.

It's worth knowing that there are several different types of 3D CAD systems, and designs produced on one aren't always compatible with another. So if you're working with one design consultancy and want to transfer your designs to another, you might have problems. It's the same when you take your final drawings to a manufacturer. There's not much you can do about this, but it's good to be aware of it.

5. Prototype

Although we may have produced some rough-and-ready prototypes during the Detail phase, this is when we create a full working prototype. Before we get to that point, though, it's helpful to know that there are different levels of prototype, each with its own purpose.

At its most basic, a prototype can consist of electronics that have been wired up to show the basic functions of how a product works. At the next level, it can be 3D printed to show a model that's the same shape and size as the finished article but doesn't have any functions; this is quick and low cost, and it's great for making early decisions about how a product looks and could be used. Then there are further levels, each using more production-grade materials and more finished levels of functionality, until we reach the point at which the prototype is almost as good as the real thing. The difference is reflected in the price: a basic prototype might cost around £100, while a full working prototype may be in the region of £10,000. One is not necessarily better than the other – it depends on what you need it for.

This is exciting. Finally you have the chance to see something that approximates to the real thing. There are all sorts of tangible features that you can only form a judgement on when you see a prototype model. You can check it out in situ, handle it in the way it's intended to be used, and see whether it's stable and secure enough for your liking.

You can also use your prototype to gain feedback from your target market. In fact, we encourage you to do this from the beginning of the design process, even as early as the concept stage. Of course, you'll get better quality feedback from a prototype than a drawing, but the problem with waiting for the prototype is that you've gone a long way through the design process before you reach that point. With concepts, you can make decisions much earlier and also see what people think about the different options. By the time you have a prototype it will be too late to make any significant changes, at least without spending more money.

The potential of 3D printing

3D printing is commonly used in prototyping now; it's no longer an emerging, experimental technology. The materials are improving and the machines are getting faster, which means that 3D printing is not far off being able to deliver meaningful economies of scale. In fact, it's almost a means of production in its own right. We work with one company that makes wearable technology for a niche market and is still in its early stages. It doesn't yet make sense for the business to manufacture large quantities, so we 3D print the non-technical elements for them. This means that the company can keep listening to its users and adapting the design, and, because there's no investment in tooling, it's cost-effective and straightforward to keep evolving the product. The unit cost is higher than if it were made on a production line and the quality isn't perfect, but for its market application it works well.

It's exciting to consider how 3D printing can lower the barrier to entry for getting a product to market. With increasing improvements in the materials used, it soon won't be possible to tell the difference between a printed part and a traditionally moulded one. It only takes a bit of imagination to think of all sorts of ways that this could transform product prototyping and manufacture in the future.

6. Optimize

This is when we start the handover to the manufacturer. The most significant element is the creation of the engineering drawings, which translate the 3D CAD model into a plan that gives the factory everything it needs to make the product. These include the intended materials, any specialist components that need to be sourced, the allowable tolerances for the parts in terms of appearance and function, and all the technical specifications. You can think of the drawings as being the instruction manual for how to produce the product.

It's common for the manufacturer to have questions and suggestions about the drawings, and there's always a lot of back and forth between us and them. They need to understand the design in detail, and, while we've thought about what manufacturing processes will be involved, there might be certain aspects that require the design to be tweaked before the production begins.

7. Certify

Many products require some form of certification before they can be sold. The standard form of certification is the UKCA mark (UK Conformity Assessed) and its EU equivalent, the CE mark. This is a technical document that you need to produce to demonstrate that your product has been designed and manufactured with the correct level of diligence. If you want to find out more you can go to the gov. uk website, which has a lot of information about the steps to take if you want to display a UKCA mark on your product.[18]

---

[18] www.gov.uk/guidance/using-the-ukca-marking

There are more specialist levels of compliance required for medical products. For these, you need to demonstrate that you've complied with the correct standards throughout the design process, not just at the end. This involves collating evidence every step of the way to show that you made the right decisions at that time. You can see why you'd need to know about this from the beginning of your product journey.

There are also special certifications for safety-critical products. We've been involved with many of these, and, in each case, we've had to identify what the relevant British and international standards are. For instance, we worked on a rescue stretcher that had to be made to certain dimensions and be capable of carrying a specific maximum weight. The certification documentation even showed how it would be tested by an external testing house. Knowing what these requirements are up front is so important, and, while I've shown certification as a later phase of work, it's actually something that you and your designer should consider from the start.

8. Manufacture

This is the final handover to the manufacturer and the point at which you will eventually take over responsibility for the next stage of your product's progress. However, before we reach that point, there are many problems for us to solve. It's easy to assume that once a product is designed the hard bit is over, and we just hand over the drawings to the factory and they go ahead and make it. The reality is that there's always a lot of back and forth between your designer and manufacturer during this phase. The factory might have questions about how to translate the design into a physical product and suggestions on how to reduce the unit cost. It's impossible to anticipate every aspect of making your product until the handover is underway – in fact, it can take three to five months until the production line is ready to go.

After these discussions, the factory sends an initial batch of part samples and we check these along with our client. The samples aren't as finessed as the final product, but they do allow for changes to the tool before it's too late. Once our client has signed off on the samples, they place an order direct with the manufacturer for whatever order quantity they've decided on.

This is an area where things can go wrong. Recently, we developed a shower head that had a rotating water jet pattern to give different shower experiences. When we received a sample back from the factory, the shower head didn't move. After taking it apart we discovered why: there was supposed to be a screw to facilitate the rotation that the manufacturer had removed to make the product quicker to assemble. To them this may have seemed like a logical thing to do, but only because they didn't understand the purpose of the design. After we explained this, they produced a corrected sample.

That's why the interface between design consultancy and factory is so important; if the two don't work closely together, you could end up with a product that doesn't work in the way that you want. In the UK this is much less likely to be an issue than in China, partly because it's easier to communicate the nuances of what you need, and partly because there aren't the same cultural differences to contend with.

In the next chapter we'll explain the steps to take when selecting your own product design consultancy. After that, you'll be ready to get started.

The main points

- ✓ Every design agency has its own process, but they tend to follow broadly similar lines to ours at ITERATE.
- ✓ First we go through a research process, the outcome of which is the identification of potential problems that need solutions.
- ✓ Next comes the creation of design concepts and their refinement.
- ✓ Now we're getting into 3D mode. We produce CAD models of the chosen concept, from which come prototypes.
- ✓ Engineering drawings, certification to ensure the product is safe, and a final handover to the manufacturer complete the design process.

10

How to Choose a
Product Designer

Choosing the right designer for your product is an important first step. You're going to be spending a lot of time with this person, and you'll be trusting them to deliver the physical manifestation of a dream that's been inside your head for a long while. Why not spend a bit of time looking at the options and weighing them up against your requirements?

I should add that there are many freelance designers and design consultancies both in the UK and around the world. The advice you'll read here isn't meant to sway you in any particular direction – it's simply to give you the information you need to make the right decision for you. Although naturally I'm proud of my own consultancy, I know it's not the best fit for all entrepreneurs or indeed their products, so my aim here is to help you pick the most appropriate partner for your needs.

Freelancers versus consultancies

There are two broad routes you can take: working with a freelance designer or working with a product design consultancy. If you're set on the consultancy route then you can skip this section, but if you're considering hiring a freelancer, it's worth understanding the pros and cons.

Freelancer pros

A freelancer could be a great starting point for you. You might only be mulling over your idea at this stage – wondering if it has 'legs' – and not wanting to commit too much money for now. Asking a freelance product designer to draw up some initial designs is a good way of dipping your toe in the water before deciding if you want to take things further. It's quick, relatively simple, and low cost.

It's not hard to find a freelancer. If you go to sites such as Upwork.com or Freelancer.com (plus others), you'll find a huge variety of skills on offer, and you can specify the expertise you're after, such as creative design, electronics, mechanical, or 3D CAD. There are so many people listed there that you'll probably find someone who suits you.

Freelancer cons

The main disadvantage with freelancers is that the one you choose is unlikely to have access to the array of skills that you'd find in a design consultancy.

Because of that, their expertise will be lacking in at least one critical area, if not more.

Not long ago we were approached by Muzhir, an inventor who had an idea for a new type of office chair. He'd already asked a freelancer to work up some visuals and these were helpful, as they gave him a good idea of how the product would look. Plus, he didn't have to spend much of his budget. But when we saw the designs he'd been given, we realized that there wasn't nearly enough detail in terms of the inner workings. To someone who wasn't a product engineer the visuals would have seemed complete, but to us it was clear that they didn't show how the chair would operate in real life. That's not to say that the drawings weren't handy for us, as they showed us what Muzhir had in his imagination, but we had to tell him that the design needed to be completely reworked. This was an unwelcome surprise, but when he understood our reasoning, he decided to work with us to get his product to manufacture.

Another downside to working with a freelancer is that you only have access to their point of view, not that of other designers in a consultancy. This is limiting when it comes to the cross-fertilization of ideas. The designers in a consultancy often work across multiple sectors, and this can result in innovative thinking. For instance, you may have noticed that some medical products, such as asthma pumps, are starting to look less functional and more visually appealing. I believe that this shift has been driven by design consultancies, which are applying a consumer aesthetic to this type of product because of their experience across different industries.

If you're still keen to work with a freelancer, then checking out their reviews is a good place to start. However, bear in mind that the reviews won't necessarily tell the whole story. They'll show whether the freelancer's clients were happy with them, which is certainly worth knowing, but what work were the reviews actually for? Was the reviewer's intent to develop a product all the way to production, or was it to just have a great CAD model that they could use to take their thinking further? The freelancer might have done a great job, but that job could be different to the one you have in mind.

In summary, a freelancer is an excellent starting point if you just want to experiment with your product idea and see what it looks like. However, it's unlikely that they'll be able to take your idea all the way to production. For that, you'll need to project manage a number of freelancers over several months, which will be a challenge if you're not an expert in all the tasks that need to be completed.

With a consultancy, on the other hand, you have access to a project team rather than only one individual. You'll benefit from a diverse creative input, as well as their engineering know-how and mechanical and electronic expertise. This means that your project can be handled by the same outfit from start to finish. A consultancy may also have external relationships that it's built up over the years, such as with investors, grant providers, marketing agencies, and legal experts. These could be invaluable when you're taking your product forward to each of the relevant stages.

How to choose a design consultancy: first steps

Given that at some point in your product journey you're almost certainly going to need the services of a consultancy, here's what to consider when creating a shortlist of who to speak to.

The type of expertise it offers

Some consultancies specialize in certain industry sectors, such as medical, consumer, electronic, wearable, or smart-related products. There's also a variation in the skills and expertise they offer. For instance, they might focus on textiles or heavy engineering, or on projects that are research or usability led. They may also have a bias towards certain aspects of the design process, such as creating visual concepts or designing for manufacture. Suppose your idea is for a medical product, and a consultancy that you're interested in has good industrial design skills but isn't able to take your product all the way to the manufacturing stage. Not only is it likely to design a product that doesn't comply with relevant medical safety standards, but you'll also have to find another resource to create your engineering drawings. Ask yourself: do this company's skills align with what I want to achieve for my product? That's the key.

Its previous experience

A consultancy's portfolio is the best place to start if you want to see what else it's done. You should be able to find this easily on its website, although some companies are better than others at showcasing their work.

When you're looking at the portfolio, try to avoid the assumption that if a consultancy hasn't already designed a product similar to yours, it's not a good fit. In reality, this rarely matters. What's far more important is that it can create products that look good, work well, and are capable of being manufactured. We once had an enquiry from someone who had an idea for a chicken coop. Had we designed one before, they asked? Our response was that it didn't matter whether we had or not, because what we would bring to the project was our engineering design expertise and not our knowledge of chickens and coops. In fact, if we had designed a chicken coop before, there might even have been a conflict of interest for us.

Its location

I've left this until last because it's usually the least important consideration. If you're keen to visit your consultancy in person, then, naturally, location is something you'll want to consider, but it would be unusual to find a company that couldn't deliver your project remotely. In fact, that's the way we do most of our work, and it means you can even work with a consultancy abroad.

Now that you understand your criteria, have a look online for any design consultancies that appear to fit them. Check out their portfolios, read reviews about them, and look at their success records. I suggest you draw up a shortlist of at least two or three because you need to be confident that the one you choose is the best fit for you.

How to choose a design consultancy: next steps

You can learn a certain amount about a consultancy online, but you'll only discover what it's really like when you talk to someone there. Here's what to look out for when you get to that stage.

How it responds to your enquiry

This starts before the first conversation. When you're on the consultancy's website, how easy is it to send an initial enquiry? Is it a simple process or are you expected to fill out a detailed questionnaire, with questions you may have no way of answering yet? In my experience, most people just want to have an informal chat at first: 'I've got this idea and I think it's a good one, but what do you think? Is it the sort of thing you could help me with?'

The quality of the initial response will tell you a lot about its approach. How long does it take someone to get back to you? Does the person seem approachable and enthusiastic? Are they willing to talk things through and give you their top-of-the-head opinions without expecting you to commit to anything? Because if they're not communicating well at the beginning when they want your business, what will it be like if problems arise later? Any product development project will encounter challenges, and often there are reasonable explanations for them, but you deserve to be kept in the loop. We've heard sad tales from people about consultancies not picking up the phone no matter how many times they called, presumably because they have other priorities or have hit technical problems that they're scared to communicate. So pay attention to how your initial enquiry is dealt with.

Also, when you're having these early conversations, it's important to talk not only to the person who responds to your enquiry but also to the members of the team you'll be working with. At the very least you should be told who they are and a bit about them. If you only communicate with the head of the consultancy or its salesperson and later find out that you don't get on with the people who'll be delivering your project, things will quickly fall apart.

Whether it questions your idea

Your dream consultancy might be one that says, 'What a fantastic idea! It's perfect, let's start straightaway!' And wouldn't that be nice? But in reality, that sort of response should raise a red flag.

A consultancy that seems happy to take your money without questioning your idea might deliver a nice-looking design, but will it translate into a marketable product? Does the product solve a problem? Would anyone want to buy it and, if so, who? Is it capable of being manufactured at a reasonable cost? These are important questions to explore right from the start, and the consultancy should be willing to challenge your assumptions. It's the expert in developing products, and the reason you've gone to it is because you don't have its knowledge and expertise. It would be unusual if your idea had no wrinkles that needed to be ironed out. An effective partner will highlight them and find ways of solving or working around them; they might even suggest a more lucrative or innovative way of designing your product than you've thought of yourself.

While you're having this conversation, it would be helpful if you talked through the aspects of designing and manufacturing a product that you've learned about in this book. If you find yourself knowing more than the consultancy about some of them, go elsewhere.

How much it understands about the processes involved

To a non-designer, a 3D printed prototype can look much like the finished article, but that doesn't mean it's been designed for injection moulding or any other manufacturing processes. Sometimes people only realize that there's a problem with their CAD model or prototype when they approach a factory. By this time they've spent a fair amount of money but have been left with a design that isn't capable of being turned into a real-life product.

We worked with one client who had an interesting idea for a bike helmet that reduced wind noise, which can be an irritation for cyclists. At the point when they approached us, they'd got as far as developing a prototype and testing it in wind tunnels. It worked well, and all that was needed was a set of engineering drawings to hand over to a manufacturer – or so they thought. However, the prototype design and materials weren't capable of being translated into a mass-manufactured product; with the methods they'd used, it would only ever be possible to make more prototypes. So even though they'd assumed that the project was almost completed, we had to rework the design. We were able to do that because many of our designers have worked in manufacturing environments in the past and have therefore had exposure to the different processes involved.

Whether it has a better idea

Although a design not being suitable for manufacture is one of the main problems we come across, another is a lack of strategic understanding about what will sell in the marketplace. We were approached by a podiatrist who wanted to create a particular type of complex shoe insert; the product already existed in the market, but she thought (correctly, as it turned out) that it would be cheaper to 3D print it. We could have run with this idea, but we also wanted to take a broader view. What our client was asking for would work, but it was still relatively low value; was there a more innovative offering that we could develop? Over several months we worked to see if we could create a bigger sales opportunity by solving the user's problem in a better and more permanent way. In the end, we created a device that used EMG (electromyography) technology; this addressed a different market need but had the potential to be far more lucrative than the original printed sole idea.

This shows the added value that the cross-functional expertise of a design consultancy can bring. If you're open to suggestions like this, you may want to have a 'can we do this better?' attitude as a criterion for the partner you choose to work with.

The external connections it has

A design consultancy can never cater to all your needs. You'll probably require a number of additional services, such as finance, marketing, and legal advice. Where your consultancy comes in is if it can point you in the right direction for these services, so it's worth asking them about its contacts when you have your initial conversations. We've helped many of our clients gain funding because of our working relationship with various funding bodies, for instance.

Questions you can ask

Here's a list of questions you might want to ask a prospective product design consultancy. It's not prescriptive, as your needs may be different to someone else's, but you can use it as a guide. The answers you receive will tell you a lot about what you need to know.

- How will you decide if it's possible to manufacture my product idea?
- Do you reckon that this product is something that would sell?
- Should I patent my idea?
- Does it seem like a technology that would infringe somebody else's patent?

- What process will you use to take my idea from concept to reality?
- What challenges have you come across when designing other people's products, and how did you overcome them?
- Can you point me in the right direction for funding options?

The proposal

After you've assessed your shortlisted consultancies on their specialisms, expertise, and communications, you can ask each of them for a proposal. This is a document that explains what you'll receive by when and how much it will cost you.

When you receive a proposal, consider how much thought the company appears to have put into it. If all they've done is drop you an email with some figures in, that's not very professional. Nor is it legally binding, as you don't have their terms and conditions. A proper proposal should summarize the background to your idea – why you want to create your product, who it's aimed at, what problem it solves – then go on to cost all the stages of the design process. You should be clear about what the consultancy will deliver at each phase, plus how much it plans to charge and when. If the proposal only gives you one figure at the end, you won't know how much you're liable for if you want to pause or cancel your project part way through. The document should also give you estimated timelines for each body of work.

Bear in mind that, at this point, the consultancy probably doesn't have enough information to give you exact costs and timings for every element of your product journey. For instance, it doesn't yet know what materials and manufacturing processes will be used, where the product will be made or from how many components. But the proposal should make it clear where more analysis needs to be done and when the costings will be available.

One option to consider, especially if your idea is particularly innovative, is to ask a consultancy only to carry out some initial research before you go any further. In this, your project manager will help you research your assumptions to see if the product would be marketable, investigate the intellectual property implications, and judge whether it's technically feasible. You might be surprised to discover that the consultancy doesn't necessarily know all this up front, but that's normal; if it claims to have all the answers, it's likely to be a warning sign.

This initial research can be invaluable in helping you to decide whether to go ahead with the project at all. We worked with one client, Sam, who had an idea for a budget car turntable; this is a revolving disc that is set in a driveway and spins a car around to make it easier to get it onto the road. Car turntables were originally developed for the luxury market, but Sam was convinced that there was room for a cheaper version to sell into the wider marketplace. We agreed it was interesting but weren't convinced it would be possible to manufacture a low-cost design, so we suggested doing a piece of research before we went any further. It turned out that the technical complexity of the product, and the safety standards it needed to comply with, would make it impossible to create a budget version. His development costs would be so high that, if he sold it for a low price, it would take him 30 years to recoup his investment. Although disappointed, he could see that the research had saved him a lot of wasted money.

Pitfalls to watch out for

There are three common failure points when it comes to working with a product designer, whether it be a freelancer or a consultancy. If you're aware of what can go wrong, you can use this not only as a screening method when you're choosing who to work with, but also as a way to help you navigate any difficulties during the road ahead.

Not designing for manufacture

This comes up time and again. We often speak to product owners who are disappointed and frustrated because they've paid for designs and drawings that look good but aren't detailed enough for a factory to work with. A usable design involves thinking from the inside out – from the interior mechanism of a product to the outer aesthetic. If your design doesn't do this, you might find that the visuals you have are of little practical value.

Related to this is when a designer develops a product that works, but after it's been produced it looks unappealing or doesn't work well for its users. The low-quality design hasn't stopped it getting to market, but the product is unlikely to sell.

Not communicating with honesty

No project is easy. By definition, your design consultancy will be creating something that's never existed before, so there are bound to be challenges along the way. Some parts of the design will need to be changed because of unforeseen problems – it's inevitable. So if your project hits some hurdles, then it's nothing to worry about, and it's certainly not a reason to ditch whoever you're working with and find someone new.

Where it is a problem, however, is if your designer doesn't communicate the situation to you and find a solution. Sometimes these conversations are difficult to have, but your designer should be as committed to the project as you are. They can't move forward with it if they're not telling you what's going on and asking you what you think.

Not designing to suit the market

A product can look amazing and work beautifully, but if it's aimed at a market that doesn't want to buy it, it won't give you a return on your investment. A designer should therefore not only be interested in designing a product but also in creating one that's likely to sell. At all stages of the journey they should be talking to you about market research, usability testing, and customer feedback, and if they're not, this is a responsibility you need to take on yourself.

The main points

- ✓ Working with a freelancer can be a good starting point if you want to visualize your idea.
- ✓ However, to take a product to manufacture, you're probably going to need a design consultancy.
- ✓ The first things to look for when choosing a consultancy are expertise, experience, and location.
- ✓ Once you start talking to people, the main elements to focus on are how that person responds to your enquiry, whether they interrogate your idea, and what their understanding is of all the stages of the design process.
- ✓ The three main pitfalls to watch out for when selecting and working with a designer are not designing a product for manufacture, not communicating with honesty, and not designing to suit your product's market.

Conclusion

'Ideas are of themselves extraordinarily valuable, but an idea is just an idea. Almost anyone can think up an idea. The thing that counts is developing it into a practical product.' So said Henry Ford, founder of the motor company. He was right, of course, and now that you know what's involved in creating a product from an idea, you're in the best possible place to make it happen for you.

The journey is not an easy one and it will test you in different ways, so you need to know why you want to do it and what your long-term vision is. Because while making a product can be a vehicle for you achieving your dreams, it can also go terribly wrong. You'll need a whole different skill set to the one that you're likely to have already, and there will be plenty of people happy to relieve you of your cash without delivering the right service. That's why you need to start with your 'why' – your own personal reason for being a product innovator. When you know that, you'll be able to make the decisions most likely to get you the results you want.

Next, you need to take a big step back from your idea. It is critical to define what problem it solves. Just because you think a product is the best solution to a problem doesn't mean it is. You can test it out by thinking more broadly: given the problem your product will solve, are there any other solutions that spring to mind? Try to be as open-minded and creative as you can – you might come up with some better ideas.

Also, who do you think will buy your product? It won't be everyone, that's for sure. If you're basing it on a problem you've had yourself, you might be tempted to think that your market is 'people like me'. But what does that mean? And are there any other customers who might buy it? Who are they? What are they like? Can you envisage them using your product and, if so, how? Again, be as objective as possible because no one else is going to be as excited about your product as you are.

Once you have your positioning sorted, you need to learn about all sorts of areas of business that you may never have considered before. Unless you're a lawyer, you probably only have a rudimentary knowledge of intellectual property. The same goes for gaining funding, picking a business model and sales strategy, deciding what manufacturer to go with, and understanding the product design process. These are all topics that I've explored with you in this book and you're now well placed to create your own product plans.

By working things through in a comprehensive way, you're doing several things: reducing your risk, making the process easier and more enjoyable, and maximizing the chances of your product being a success. When you know from the start what you're taking on, you're less likely to run out of money and time and make mistakes that cost you dearly. You'll also feel more in control; there's nothing like having some knowledge to give you confidence, and it's fun to learn new things. But the most important outcome of reading this book is that you'll now be thinking strategically about all the steps on the product development journey, which means that your product will be what you want it to be.

Despite all the products I've seen through to completion, I've never lost the excitement of seeing the latest one hit the market. It's a buzz that you'll feel, too, when yours reaches that point. Nothing compares to the satisfaction of watching your creation make its way from idea to prototype to finished article and seeing it bought and used by eager customers. You can say, 'That's my product!'

Good luck with your venture – may your product bring you everything you hope for and more.

Index

The Author

Gethin Roberts has over 15 years' experience in developing new products in the medical, industrial, and consumer sectors. He started his career as an in-house design engineer, which gave him hands-on experience of designing products for manufacture. It also meant that he was involved in the various commercial aspects of developing new products.

He's now Managing Director of ITERATE, a dynamic product design consultancy that blends creative and technical expertise to develop products from concepts all the way through to production. Gethin's master's degree in Rapid Product Development taught him that many businesses are slow to respond to market demands; this led him to create the Rapid Development Product Pathway for his business, which focuses on removing the barriers that stop new products getting to market.

As a consultant on the Welsh Government's SMART Productivity and Design Programme, Gethin has gained huge insights into an array of product sectors. From multi-million-pound companies to small start-ups, he's seen it all. He's also lectured at the University of the West of England, supporting its product design faculty and helping students with design submissions to the annual Royal Society of Arts competition.

When not working with clients to help them create plans for their product development, poring over CAD drawings, or presenting his consultancy's latest 3D-printed prototypes, Gethin enjoys spending time with his wife and two daughters.

You can discover more about ITERATE at www.iterate-uk.com.

Acknowledgements

I would like to thank the team at ITERATE, past and present, for your hard work, creativity, and persistence when helping to bring new products to life for our customers!

I am also very grateful to Ginny Carter for the help she has provided in the creation of this book.

But most importantly, I would like to thank my family and friends for their unwavering support throughout my business career.